TALES OF McKINLEYVILLE

Big Doin's At The Chinese Baptist Church

A Novel by
PERRY BRADFORD-WILSON

with photographs by
Brandi Easter

Storyteller Press
in association with
Page One Publishers & Bookworks, Inc.
Eureka, California

© 1998 by Perry Bradford-Wilson

All rights reserved under International and Pan-American Copyright Conventions. Without limiting the rights under copyright reserved above, no part of this book may be reproduced or transmitted in any form or by any means, electronic or mechanical, including photocopying, recording, or by any information storage and retrieval system, without permission in writing from the author.

Published in the United States by

Storyteller Press

in association with
Page One Publishers & Bookworks, Inc.
P.O. Box 6606
Eureka, CA 95502-6606

ISBN 1-880053-02-0
First Edition, November 1998

Manufactured in the United States Of America by Eureka Printing, Eureka, CA. **BUY LOCAL.**
Library of Congress Cataloging-in-Publication Data is available from the publisher.
Book design & Map illustration by Perry Bradford-Wilson

PUBLISHER'S NOTE

This book is a work of fiction. Names, characters, places, and incidents are either products of the author's imagination or are used fictitiously. Any resemblance to actual events, locales or persons, living or dead, is entirely coincidental.

Shorter versions of "The Promotion Party," "The Eternal Ant," "Our Great President McKinley," "The True Story Of Who's Buried In McKinley's Tomb," "The Trouble With Bubba's House," "The Wild and Untamed Emu," "Big Doin's At The Chinese Baptist Church," "Bubba's Posse On The Scent," and "Our Conclusion" have appeared previously in serial form in *Comic Relief Magazine*.

A Table of Contents

Big Doin's At The Chinese Baptist Church...........5

In which we are introduced to Huck and Bubba and Huck's Secret Plan to recover a family hair-loom extraordinaire is revealed. We also learn a bit about the history of McKinleyville, its citizens, and the story of a neighboring community's statue of a doomed President.

The Promotion; The Eternal Ant; Our Great President McKinley; The True Story Of Who's Buried In McKinley's Tomb; The Trouble With Bubba's House; The Wild and Untamed Emu; Big Doin's At The Chinese Baptist Church; Bubba's Posse On The Scent; Our Conclusion

The Return Of The Teapot Dome.......................67

In which a good boy goes bad, Huck runs for public office, the tale of the HestonQuest is told, the town's black widow stalks new prey, a nearby mountain is climbed, and we are told the story of Bob Thalia and his muse.

A Good Boy Gone Bad; Politics Is As Politics Does; Tales From The Mighty Groove Of The Last Rainbow Commune; McKinleyville's Foremost Man Of Letters; The Very First Mister Fletcher; The Fall From The Top Of The World; Why Frying Pans Are Not Good For Disciplining Children; Huck Looks For Protection; The Return Of The Teapot Dome; Our Conclusion

The Marriage Proposal......................................141

In which Huck finally decides what to do with his life, love letters arrive from Hollywood, Bubba finds the perfect mate, and the whereabouts of the infamous Hunsey Bourcarte are finally revealed.

Death By Party Game; The Best Supporting Actress Comes To Humboldt County; The Decline and Sudden Fall Of Bubba Puhzz; The Marriage Proposal; Twenty-Two Days Of The Dog; A Letter Arrives; Where's Hunsey Bourcarte?; Tales Of Humboldt Babylon; The Bachelor Party; Dear John

Epilogue..221

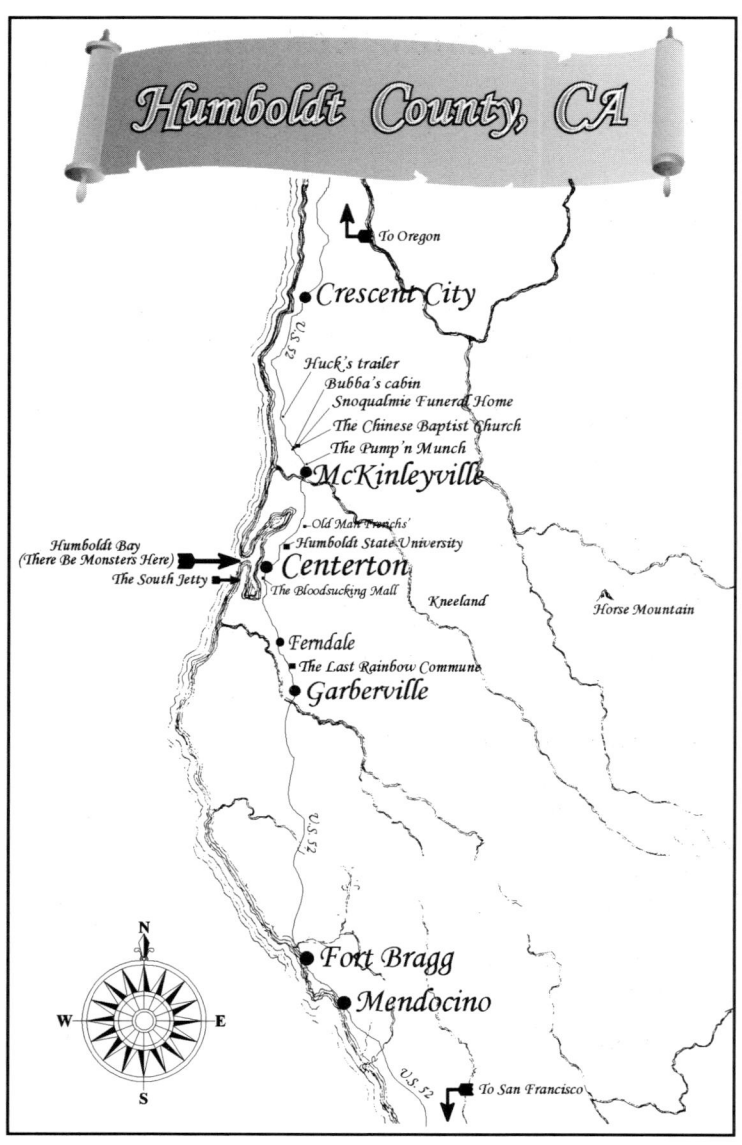

Big Doin's At The Chinese Baptist Church

I
The Promotion
In which Bubba is exalted and Huck sets his Secret Plan in motion

The unexpected and undeserved elevation of his brother to new heights of responsibility was the catalyst that finally set Huck Puhzz's Secret Plan into motion.

It all started on a fateful Tuesday in July when Huck's brother Bubba was promoted to the exalted position of night manager at the Pump'n Munch.

Huck, who is the principal character in our tale, was sitting in his barcalounger sipping a Bud and watching the daytime version of his favorite TV show, *Wheel Of Fortune*, when Bubba called him to spread the good news. He didn't want to get up to answer the phone at first, but when he did he was glad that he'd made the effort. Oh, he wasn't all that happy about his brother's promotion - it was just one more thing for Bubba to lord over him - but there was going to be a party. That probably meant free beer, free chips, and maybe even a free tin of chew. More importantly, however, it was the perfect opportunity to implement his Secret Plan.

Bubba had dreamed about the night manager

job at the gas station & convenience store throughout the eight years he had worked as its stock room clerk and now - finally - he could call it his own. Most crucial to Huck's Secret Plan, Bubba had decided to throw a party, as he was wont to do whenever he got good news. Not an expensive party, mind, but Bubba could afford a little party considering he was getting a raise from $4.25 an hour to $5.50. Earlier that morning, Bubba told Huck on the phone, he had gotten a phone call from Truman Krantz, the owner of the Pump'n Munch franchise. Truman told him that Willie Horton had quit his job as the night manager. ("Don't confuse me with *that other* Willie Horton," Willie was always reminding Bubba, although Bubba had no idea who *that other* Willie Horton was). Willie, it seemed, was moving to Centerton to be a bag boy at the new Wal-Mart, so Bubba was hereby promoted to the night shift. He was supposed to stop by at Truman's house before two o'clock that afternoon to pick up his own set of keys. He'd had to double-check that with Truman. Really? His own set of keys? Yup, his own set of keys.

This Tuesday was the second of the month and since Huck had to go to town to pick up his unemployment and disability checks anyway he decided to make a day of it. He got dressed in his hardly-faded blue jeans and a completely clean shirt (as opposed to picking the shirt with the least offensive smell off the dirty clothes pile and wearing it) and even brushed his hair. Ever since Huck had thrown out his back pulling chain down at the mill he'd spent most days just sitting here, mending. It was painful in more ways than one, because he'd always made fun of how he made three times as much money as Bubba ever did, and when he got put on disability Bubba took every opportunity to turn the tables. Huck could move around a lot better these days, although he didn't admit it to many people, and a party (and his Secret Plan) was as good an excuse as any to do the day up right.

It took him a few minutes to lock up the mobile home because the blocks it sat on had shifted and the door didn't close so well anymore. He got down on all fours and peered under the deck to see if he could make out Whizzer in case the aging mutt wanted to go to town too, but the unmoving lump in the dark under the back of the mobile didn't respond to his calls and whistles. So what, let the damn hound stay home, he thought. It was a trial hefting himself up into his pickup truck cab, trying to go easy on his back but banging his head on the gun rack in the process. The day was sunny, warm but not hot, and Huck had a feeling that his bad spell was ending, that this was going to be the best day he'd had in a long long time. Things were gonna start working his way, and he felt so lucky he decided right there and then he was going to buy double his usual number of lottery tickets. Yep, things were getting better for good ol' Huck Puhzz. Of course, Huck had never been very good at predicting the future.

The truck started on the fourth try and jumped into gear, hopping a rut in the driveway and then rattling down to US 52. The radio only got one station, but it was one of those stations where all they did was talk about politicians' sexual affairs and which foreigners were fighting in some country he had never heard of, so he just sang Garth Brooks tunes to himself. He had his 2-60 air conditioning going - two windows open at sixty miles an hour - and the shadows of the elms that lined the highway alternated with the rays of the noonday sun through the only-slightly-cracked windshield. All in all it wasn't a bad weather day for Humboldt County.

Huck hadn't been out driving since Saturday, which was his night on the Neighborhood Watch looking for skulkers. He wasn't the sort to naturally volunteer for things, but the Neighborhood Watch paid for his gas and for keeping his sidearm in clean and well-loaded shape, so he always drove around for about an hour or two on Saturday nights looking for shady characters and other suspicious-looking individuals before stopping off at the Pump'n Munch and buying a six-pack and a tin from Bubba. Afterwards he'd drive slowly home, only stopping occasionally to drink a beer and take a leak at the side of the road, the whole time keeping his eyes peeled for them skulkers.

Today he was driving fast, and his mind was racing even faster. After the first pieces of his Secret

Plan were in place he was going down to the Pump'n Munch and he was gonna start in on Bubba. This was going to take every iota of Huck's smarts (a limited resource at best) if he was going to pull it off. But if tonight went the way Huck planned it was going to mean much more than just a party and a few free beers. It would mean the restoration to glory of the greatest possession in Puhzz family history.

II
The Eternal Ant
In which we are told the story of the most amazing timepiece in history

Huck's family never had much in the way of 'hair-looms' (as Momma Puhzz called them) but it did have one legacy that had been passed down from generation to generation. Gramma Puhzz had been the richest of the Puhzz clan, with a big ol' house with four bedrooms and a 'conservatory,' which meant a room with some big windows, a few plants, and the piano. Nobody knew how to play the piano except for Gramma Puhzz. When they were just boys, Huck and Bubba would visit her and she would play songs from *Your Hit Parade* after supper in the evenings. They knew 'Moonlight Bay' and 'Accentuate The Positive' and other songs that had great parts for growing young men to sing back-up on while their Gramma sang the main words, sort of like a family version of a barbershop quartet.

The piano was already used when Gramma bought it. It was an upright with a worn finish and a few sticky keys, but she always kept it polished and set all of her cherished little porcelain dogs and cats on top of it, and right in the center, underneath her collection of spoons, was the clock.

Not to digress, but Gramma's collection of spoons was something to behold. She had spoons from sixteen states, with little shields on the handles that said where they were from. Huck's favorite was the one from Little America, Wyoming, because he thought a name like Little America was pretty keen. Whenever the family went traveling they always bought Gramma more spoons and one year Bubba had made a rack for them in wood shop out of a few pieces of leftover oak. After that they always hung right above the piano and Huck always read the words 'Little America' on his favorite spoon right away whenever he came into the room. Then he would check out the clock.

The clock was the 'hair-loom extraordinaire,' according to Momma, mostly because it had a story to go with it. Sweet Mary Christiansen, the boys' great-great-grandmomma, had originally owned it way back in the year 1863. At some time between then and when Huck's Gramma came into possession of it, something unusual happened to that clock. An ant had crawled up into the clock's interior through some crack that in all the intervening years no one had ever been able to locate (although Huck and Bubba had tried on numerous occasions.) Then that ant for no reason discernible had worked it's way carefully out onto the sweeping second hand. There, just an inch or so from the end, it had up and died.

Now a dead ant isn't much to get excited about, but the ant, you see, had stuck to the second hand. It swept around inside the clock from twelve to twelve every damn minute. And it had done just that for at least forty-five years according to Gramma. Every morning Gramma wound up the clock and kept that ant moving around and around the clockface and it hadn't stopped moving in the almost half century Gramma had owned the clock.

Gramma was modest about it and said the clock was just 'a conversation piece.' Momma crowed about how Gramma ought to send it to *Ripley's Believe It Or Not* or some newspaper and maybe sell the clock and make a bunch of money. Gramma said no one would want an old clock with a dead ant in it, but Momma loved that clock and made her promise she wouldn't ever throw it away and instead would keep it as a 'hair-loom extraordinaire' for the boys. And that's how Huck was going to end up with it, sort of.

He hadn't exactly gotten his hands on it yet. That was because when Gramma died Bubba had got it first.

Bubba was exactly nine months older than Huck, not that that had anything to do with anything, and when Gramma died they'd had to divvy up her stuff. Aunt Clarice had gotten most of the good furniture because Momma couldn't use it at the convalescent home and the house had to be sold to pay the bank and for Gramma's funereal expenses. For the most part that left a bunch of nick knacks and old clothes that smelled like cedar chests. Included were Gramma's old shotgun, Great-Grampa Puhzz's civil war sword, the spoon collection and the clock.

These last four items, it was decided, Huck and Bubba would split amongst themselves (along with the nick knacks and smelly clothes... maybe it was moth balls that they smelled like, not a cedar chest, but they were still pretty foul.) Each of the boys would get two. They just had to decide which two they wanted. Well, Huck had stared at the ceiling in bed agonizing over this one for hours.

The shotgun was pretty practical, for obvious reasons. The civil war sword was a 'hair-loom' that, while not 'extraordinaire,' was still awfully cool. Huck figured it would be a waste of a choice if he picked the spoons since he could practically have them by default on account of Bubba didn't really want them. On the other hand, he really liked the one that read 'Little America.' And then there was the clock, the only timepiece in Humboldt County that told the time by ant.

Big Doin's At The Chinese Baptist Church

  As boys Huck and Bubba had gotten along about as well as brothers do, having the occasional fight and knocking out the occasional teeth. They were friends more or less, and were used to getting drunk together and telling each other stories of imagined sexual conquests. Bubba was frequently surrounded by his posse (more on them later) but Huck pretty much got along with them. As brothers the two of them had always been fairly successful aside from your typical sibling rivalry. At least until the day they'd had to divvy up Gramma's stuff.
  In the end Huck had decided on the shotgun and the spoon collection and Bubba had hauled off with the sword and the clock. For the first few days Huck had been happy with his choice, taking Whizzer and the shotgun out into the forest above Route 36 and hunting quail. The buckshot sort-of perforated the quail and sometimes you had to spit out a few shot during dinner (maybe rubbing 'em around first with your tongue to exercise your gums), but you could knock off two or three birds in a single gunshot if you aimed right. And the spoons, well they hung on the wall over the TV where Huck could read 'Little America' right above Vanna White's head any time he wanted to. At first everything was copacetic. But after a while he began to think differently.
  The sword was just a sword as far as Huck was concerned, but the clock was the only one of its kind. He knew down deep that Bubba didn't at all

understand how special the clock really was and had no comprehension at all of the value of the thing. Whenever Huck wandered over to Bubba's cabin to split a twelve-pack he'd see him using the clock to tell time! Bubba never even looked at the ant. Huck had inherited his Momma's passion for the timepiece and was shocked by his brother's indifference. Over time he grew to resent Bubba and his self-righteous presumptive taking-hair-looms-for-granted smugness. He imagined Gramma turning over in her grave, but then he remembered Gramma didn't think all that much of the clock either, so he imagined Momma turning over in her bed at the convalescent home. It was simply a travesty.

So Huck had decided to liberate the clock.

It wasn't stealing, mind, because he and Bubba were family, and when you steal from family it's always more like extended borrowing. The clock should be with someone who appreciated it for what it was, and Bubba obviously did not. So this was not a theft - it was a liberation, a coming home of the clock, so to speak. Huck was going to put it on top of the finest piece of furniture he had - his TV - right where it belonged under the spoons. And the process of this liberation he now referred to as his "Secret Plan."

Huck was essentially an honest man, but he wasn't new at skullduggery. This wasn't the first time he had 'liberated' an unappreciated masterwork. Once, many years before, he had attempted to return glory to yet another 'hair-loom extraordinaire.' It had taken careful planning, the right tools, and the help of a key player. But with all cylinders firing, Huck had once been a part of the greatest restoration to glory ever seen in the history of the great town of McKinleyville.

III
Our Great President McKinley
In which we learn the history of the great statue and of the town's great shame

The Great McKinleynapping took place the year after Huck dropped out of high school.

He and Bubba had lived in McKinleyville for a hair over thirty years, ever since the mill in Pepperwood closed. McKinleyville wasn't as fancy as Centerton, with a mall and all, but the rent was cheap and the air was clean and Huck figured he had it twice as good as those people in the big city who breathed all that foul air and lived in traffic jams. So he was pretty happy all in all. In fact, there was only one reason a person could possibly be embarrassed about living in McKinleyville.

The town of McKinleyville was founded in 1897 and named after the brand-spankin' new President of the United States, a fellow by the name of William McKinley. In 1901, as the story was told to all the local children, that very nice fellow was shot by some dastardly evildoer and the city fathers of McKinleyville decided to memorialize a fallen hero by commissioning a statue of the late President for the town plaza. A metalworker and sculptor by the name of Copperthwaite Smith from San Francisco was commissioned to create this piece of memorial art. Work was started on it immediately at Smith's studio in the City. Copperthwaite was a fine artist, and he used dozens of photographs to achieve a stunning likeness of the bejoweled ex-President.

Such fine art takes time, and it was only after many months of painstaking sculpture that the statue was ready. Finally satisfied with it, Copperthwaite loaded it up on a wagon, joined by some fellow metalworkers. (A note aside; one of the gentlemen hauling the statue was named Ayn, which was strange because you don't hear of many men named Ayn. Then again, you hear of even fewer named Copperthwaite, so I suppose the point is moot.) With the noble President loaded on the wagon they all started out for McKinleyville.

In those days it wasn't just a five hour drive from San Francisco to McKinleyville like it is today (well, five hours if you keep it at 75 miles per hour the whole way except for when you're going through the well-known speed trap at Leggett). Nope, in those days it was a three day wagon ride on dusty roads and over steep mountains, and what with a big old heavy statue of President McKinley loaded in the

Big Doin's At The Chinese Baptist Church

back of the wagon it took even longer. Copperthwaite Smith had wired ahead to McKinleyville to announce that he was coming and the townspeople had gussied up the town with streamers and balloons in anticipation of the unveiling of the statue. But as the days passed and the statue didn't show up the citizenry got, shall we say, a trifle put out.

The straw that broke the camel's back (or maybe it's axle would be a more accurate description) is when the wagon bearing the statue broke down smack dab in the middle of the town plaza in Centerton. Copperthwaite Smith was tired and dirty after six grueling days hauling the dense metal President up and down the redwood-covered mountainsides, so he sent some of his buddies (including Ayn) onward to McKinleyville to see if he could get some help from its residents in taking the statue the rest of the way.

The people of McKinleyville, on the other hand, were not very happy with Mister Copperthwaite Smith after all the delays. The streamers they'd put up had all fallen down, kids had popped most of the balloons and now the Mayor was away on a fishing trip. Besides, they had come to the decision that they were never all that happy with the Presidency of Mister William McKinley either and it was probably not such a bad idea that he'd been shot. So they told Mr. Smith's buddies that they'd changed their minds and didn't want the statue anymore.

Copperthwaite Smith was so angry when he heard this that he just dumped that statue of President William McKinley right there in the middle of the plaza at Centerton and, after mending his wagon, went home to San Francisco where he and his buddies wouldn't have to put up with - and I use his terminology - 'stupid country bumpkins.'

And that's how McKinleyville's statue of its namesake wound up decorating Centerton's town plaza. The Centerton folk didn't mind the "gift," although the public works department never made much effort to clean the bird droppings off of the President.

The story was kind of funny at first, until you went to a football game between Centerton High and McKinleyville High and those damn Centerton brats would make smartass jokes about the statue and about the general intelligence of their statue-less rivals, jokes that will not be repeated here for the sake of common decency. Suffice it to say that, over the years, the statue of William McKinley became quite a sore subject for the people of McKinleyville.

So when Huck Puhzz dropped out of High School just halfway through his freshman year he and a friend decided to cap their academic careers with an act that would benefit everyone in their home town; the long-awaited restoration of the town's glory and honor.

Big Doin's At The Chinese Baptist Church

"And that's how McKinleyville's statue of its namesake wound up decorating Centerton's town plaza."
page 18

IV
The True Story Of Who's Buried In McKinley's Tomb
In which the details of the Great McKinleynapping unfold

Actually, Huck wasn't the mastermind behind the Great McKinleynapping. Of course, Huck had never been the mastermind behind anything on account of the fact he rarely thought things up on his own - except his Secret Plan, and the brilliance of that particular operation will be revealed in good time. The rescue of the wayward statue of the good President was more accurately the idea of the coolest guy at McKinleyville High, one Hunsey Bourcarte. Throughout school Hunsey had always been a friend of Huck's, mostly because Hunsey never had a problem getting a keg of beer. Huck and Hunsey had met in 4H and solidified their friendship when they went up to Cobb Mountain to paint a big 76 on the electric company's reflector dish (because Hunsey, if he had graduated, would have done so with the class of '76.) They got caught that time, unfortunately, because Hunsey left a ladder and several paint brushes on the scene, all of which had clearly stenciled on their sides 'Bourcarte.' Their further adventures had gone much better. And, it should be said, Hunsey was especially renowned for his power over the opposite sex, which made being friends with him all the more important to Huck's reputation.

Big Doin's At The Chinese Baptist Church

After thinking for a very long time about how to celebrate his new freedom from High School, Hunsey had decided to bring the Great Statue Of President McKinley home to McKinleyville, and the idea seemed perfectly glorious to Huck. After all, this wasn't like most of the mischief they'd gotten into in their lives, poaching deer and stealing beers. This was a service to their hometown neighbors, a patriotic thing, and besides the statue was rightly theirs anyway.

Hunsey showed up the night of the McKinleynapping at Huck's place wearing a black t-shirt and a pair of denim overalls (which was nothing special, because that's what he always wore.) Huck dressed just the same and they started out for Centerton in the Bourcartemobile, a beat up old mostly-primer-and-putty Ford truck Hunsey had bought from a junk yard for $30 and fixed up just enough so that it would start almost every time and actually move occasionally.

The trip to Centerton went smoothly thanks to their youthful enthusiasm, but the wait to steal the statue hadn't gone as well. First, they'd had to hide behind Don's Rent-All until the police changed shift (the late shift sort of kept their patrols to within a mile or less of the Happy Kup.) Then they had to wait until John Kirby, the janitor, had finished up mopping up the Bank Of America. Huck drank a couple of beers on the way over to calm his nerves. While they waited he knocked back an occasional extra to make sure he maintained the effect. Eventually he had to use the bathroom something fierce. Hunsey kept having to drive them all the way to the other side of town to the Happy Kup (dangerous since it was, as noted, enemy territory) to use the only 24 hour restroom in Centerton. Hunsey wanted Huck to just pee on the side of Don's Rent-All, but Huck said he was raised by his Grandma right, and peeing in the woods was one thing and doing it on a building was quite another. Meanwhile, in order to keep from falling asleep on their vigil, every time Huck visited the restroom at the Happy Kup Hunsey had a mug of steaming hot java.

It doesn't take a rocket scientist to predict that by one a.m. Huck was so drunk he couldn't tell the difference between Hunsey and the statue. And Hunsey, well, he was so wired from all that hot joe that as he steadied the statue on the dolly they'd brought it looked like good ol' President McKinley was having epileptic seizures.

Nonetheless, the great statue made it from its concrete base to the back of the Bourcartemobile without any kinks developing in the plan. The two boys stood at the side of the truck, admiring their work and the way the President towered above the truck cab, his arm raised almost as if he was campaigning. It was then that Hunsey realized that the road back to McKinleyville led straight past the Happy Kup and the eyes of the police officers therein. The likelihood that even the blindest of them would miss the statue as it rode by, teetering high above the Bourcartemobile, was slim. Even Huck could see that.

Huck was of the opinion that they should just drive past the Happy Kup real fast, but Hunsey put on his thinking cap (literally, a baseball cap he owned that he said kept his brain warmer) and had a better idea. There was an alternate route back to Highway 36, one that he'd taken many times in his youth by bicycle delivering newspapers to greater Centerton. It led right through the back forty at Old Man Frerich's ranch. And Hunsey was "pretty sure" the old track was wide enough for the truck. So he fired up the Bourcartemobile and Hunsey, Huck, and President McKinley headed for the ranch.

To fully appreciate what happened next a slight bit of background is necessary. Ol' Man Frerichs hated the city of Centerton (for good cause, but that's somebody else's story.) He refused to use any of the city public services, which it so happened included water and sewer. Therefore Ol' Man Frerichs had a well and a septic tank. That isn't so unusual in itself except that they weren't a very good well or septic tank, so Ol' Man Frerichs had to buy bottled water when the well went dry and he had to use an old fashioned outhouse when the septic tank or leaching lines clogged up.

To make a long and painful story short, the Bourcartemobile impacted the side of Ol' Man Frerichs' outhouse with enough force to push it about twelve feet from its moorings. The back wheel of the truck got caught on the edge of the pit over which the outhouse had once rested (and if you don't know what the pit is, child, then never mind) and the bed started to tilt.

Hunsey and Huck were out and on their feet inspecting the damage to the truck and things didn't look good. The tire on one side was flat and the opposite wheel hung precariously over open space. Huck was about to suggest they hoof it when President McKinley started his slide. At first it was just a small movement, accompanied by a little scraping sound. Then with the sorta screechy sound of metal-on-metal the President started to slide faster and before Huck or Hunsey could do a thing he'd taken a header over the tailgate and vanished into the pit.

The boys would probably have left right then and there if Ol' Man Frerichs' light hadn't have popped on. The old man's head stuck out and the beam from his flashlight started swarming all over the place. He was in a terrycloth robe, slippers that Huck could've sworn had little faces on the toes, and he had a rifle in the hand opposite the flashlight.

Hunsey shushed Huck and they squirmed around the front of the truck and hid behind a big tree (which, coincidentally, hid Ol' Man Frerichs pump which he had out on account of his septic tank being stopped up, as usual.) The Ol' Man came up slow to the edge of the pit where his outhouse used to sit. His flashlight swept the depths below the hang-

Big Doin's At The Chinese Baptist Church

ing rear-end of the Bourcartemobile. And there, dimly in the spotlight, he saw the President.

"Hello! Who ist dat? Ahr you alright?!" the old man had cried. When the President didn't move the Ol' Man had edged closer, maybe thinking some poor drunk driver was passed out down there or something, and that's when the bank gave way and he joined the President in, as they say, the soup.

When Sheriff Wadd arrived in response to Old Lady Frerichs' call he found Huck dangling a branch to the rancher, who was still swimming in the pit below. Hunsey and Huck were arrested for trespassing and for vandalism of city property. The Centerton judge eventually let them off with a stern warning (after all, they were only fifteen). Even though they had failed to bring the President home to McKinleyville they were revered in their hometown as heroes for their daring actions. After all, the townspeople didn't want the damn statue back. They just wanted to get even with Centerton for all those years of abuse, and dumping the Centerton Plaza statue in an outhouse was exactly the sort of revenge they had been dreaming of for decades (no one ever accused these people of having very good imaginations.) Forever more in McKinleyville the area out back of Ol' Man Frerichs' ranch in Centerton was known as 'McKinley's Tomb.' Every time the Centerton brats tried to make fun of the Wildcats at a football game you just had to ask "So, who's buried in McKinley's Tomb?" and they'd quiet up but fast.

So although things went terribly wrong (as far as the original plan went), Huck and Hunsey had indeed restored their town's honor and glory and were loved and respected by their fellow citizens.

Old Man Frerich's feelings about the matter are, of course, a totally different story.

V
The Trouble With Bubba's House
In which Huck's Secret Plan meets with adversity

A veteran of the Great McKinleynapping, therefore, Huck was no stranger to dangerous missions. His Secret Plan to liberate his Grandma's clock had been much better thought out than his other brilliant schemes (for instance, Huck had decided to drink no beer, and stay strictly on paved roads.) The trickiest part was going to be making sure Bubba wasn't around during the actual liberation.

Bubba, as has been noted, worked at the Pump'n Munch for the past eight years. Although he had always been a stock room clerk, the opportunity to be his own boss for a night at a time had come up now and then, especially when the previous night manager, Willie Horton, had a date and decided not to show up for work. On those occasions Bubba had been in charge, with all of the duties and responsibilities of an actual night manager

Big Doin's At The Chinese Baptist Church

excepting the fact he didn't have a key. Not being completely stupid, Bubba had taken liberal advantage of these nights of responsibility. He told Huck it was 'manager's privilege' and he would proceed to eat and drink the inventory, fill his truck with gas, and at least once a night run home and leave one of the 'posse' in charge (introductions to the 'posse' will come later.)

If Truman Krantz, the owner of the Pump'n Munch franchise, had known Bubba sometimes deserted his post and left non-employees watching the place, he probably would've fired the boy outright, much less promoted him to night manager. But no one told Truman on account of all the free beer and stuff they always got from Bubba for keeping their traps shut.

Basically, to make his Secret Plan happen here was the deal; Huck had to make sure Bubba didn't take one of his AWOL trips home right at the moment Huck was liberating the clock. And that was why the big promotion party was going to come in right handy.

Once he got into town Huck bought his weekly lotto tickets (he didn't buy them from Bubba because he thought that would be bad luck) and hung out with Andy Peterson for a few minutes in front of the gun cabinet at the Ace Hardware, each of them pretending they knew a lot more about guns than they actually did. "Oh, they stopped makin' that .22 in 1975," one would say, and the other would say, "But the 9 mil was a deader aim," whilst they looked longingly at a big ol' .44 that had been gathering dust in the cabinet for six years. Later he bought a bottle of Black Velvet at the Safeway (Bubba's favorite liquor - and one which was not stocked at the Pump'n Munch) and then made his way across town.

The posse was already forming on the bench in front of the store talking about auto parts. Big Kenny, who was going on 400 pounds, sat at one end. Hampton and Sammy both sat on the other end for ballast. The three of them would most likely sit out there gabbing until the gas fumes got the better of them and then they'd go in and hit Bubba up for beers. Larry and his son Little Larry would both be there as soon as the mill shut down for the night, but Huck expected to be long gone by that time.

He said "hey" to the guys and then went in and congratulated Bubba. They talked about how far they'd come in life since High School and how proud Momma would be of Bubba when she heard the news next weekend. Lately they hadn't talked much. Most of the time these days they just tried to one-up each other until they got fighting mad and one of them went home. But now they found themselves reminiscing just like good brothers are supposed to do. Huck might have admitted to himself he sorta missed these sorts of conversations, but the Secret Plan was too busy occupying his brain. Bubba sprang for a couple of cokes (or, to be more accurate, Truman Krantz did). The moment was the perfect opportu-

Big Doin's At The Chinese Baptist Church

nity for Huck to pop the Black Velvet onto the counter and offer it to Bubba as a promotion-celebration present. The timing was perfect. Bubba almost got teary-eyed at it, moved 'n all that his brother cared so much.

Boy, had Huck fooled him.

In fact, everything was going exactly to plan until the blurry old black & white TV over the cash register finished rolling the credits to *Jeopardy* and the opening theme of *Wheel Of Fortune* suddenly started up. Standing next to Pat Sajak Huck could see the queen of the game show, Vanna White, in all her glorious black & whiteness. To say that he was mesmerized is an understatement. He stood there, blocking half the front counter of the Pump'n Munch, while Susan from Ohio spun the Wheel and bought an 'E.' When Bubba chased the pimple-faced kid with the phony I.D. out of the store, Huck was so entranced by Jack from Alabama (who asked for an 'S' and got four of them) that he didn't even notice. He didn't see Big Kenny, Hampton, Sammy, and both Larrys come in and plant themselves at the donut bar because Ophelia from New York was jumpin' up and down and screaming because she had correctly guessed 'The Shape Of Things To Come.' Only when the credits wound down and an ad for feminine hygiene products came on did Huck finally realize that it had gotten dark outside.

You have to give the boy credit that he made up his ground quickly. He grabbed a stack of styrofoam cups from the coffee area and brought them over to the posse, filling each with about two shots worth of the whiskey he had brought. The guys had already inhaled almost a six-pack of beer each, so Huck hoped this was going to ice their cakes. Bubba passed around the whiskey while the Larrys unwrapped a king's ransom in Ho Hos and Ding Dongs, and the partying got started in earnest. In ten minutes the whiskey bottle was empty and phase two of Huck's cunning plan was ready to go into motion.

"Hey, boys, how 'bout I pop round to the Safeway for another bottle?" he asked. There was a chorus of affirmative-sounding noises and Bubba slapped him on the back, so Huck got up and walked boldly out of the Pump'n Munch and jumped into his truck heading, presumably, for the Safeway store.

Of course, this was the clever part of Huck's plan. Instead of going to the Safeway, he was headed directly for Bubba's house and the prized family heirloom that waited within. If he could get the clock, drop it off at his trailer, get to the Safeway and buy another bottle of Black Velvet in a short enough time the posse would never notice it had taken so long, at least not as drunk as they were.

He flicked on the high beams to see his way in the countryside night better, then quickly forgot that he had done so and couldn't figure out why all the city cars coming the opposite direction kept honking and flicking their lights at him. His mind was so focused on his Secret Plan that he didn't even

Big Doin's At The Chinese Baptist Church

bother to look for skulkers.

About three miles up US 52 he pulled off on a gravel road and turned off his lights. There was just enough moonlight that he could make out the silhouette of the squat cabin that Bubba called home. During the day he could have seen the peeling paint and patch-up tarpaper that decorated its sides, but tonight it was just a black square against the sky. He killed the engine about ten yards from the building, got the rusted flashlight from the glove compartment (he had brought all the tools necessary), and then he creeped stealthily up to the front door.

Which was locked.

This was certainly not a situation that Huck had been prepared for, because the door was almost always unlocked. It's not that Bubba was careless, lax, or naive about the need for security. It was that Bubba came home drunk about four nights a week and he was afraid he wouldn't be able to locate his keys, so he left the house unlocked all the time. Huck had no way of knowing that Bubba, after stopping by Truman Krantz's house that afternoon to pick up the keys to the Pump'n Munch, had come home before going to work. And Huck had no way of knowing that Bubba was so enamoured by the responsibility of the store keys that he had elected to lock the front door of the cabin as he left for work. He was a manager now, Bubba had decided, and managers had keys. And managers had keys because they locked doors.

The only other likely means of entrance into Bubba's cabin was the bathroom window. Huck knew this because he had tried to help Bubba fix the window clasp one day, but the frame had been painted over so many times that the thick paint rose higher than the bottom of the clasp and it wouldn't turn anymore. So Huck walked with Injun feet around the house to the bathroom.

The window was slightly high, but Huck could stand level with it if he stood on the garden faucet, so he climbed up and balanced on the ball of his right foot. He got some leverage by pushing off the faucet handle with the other foot. Sitting around home most days and all he wasn't in the best of shape, but he could feel the window starting to give and he pushed even harder. Suddenly with one thunder-and-lightning crack the whole frame gave way and the entire window, Huck traveling along with it, fell into Bubba's bathtub. The window shattered as it came into contact with the hot water knob and the side of the tub, and broken glass flew into the air like hail in reverse.

Huck didn't move for a few moments after everything settled. First he checked to make sure he was alive and checked to make sure he wasn't bleeding in spurts from some severed artery. Then he surveyed the field of broken glass and splintered wood and decided that it would be okay to stand up if he was really careful. There were lots of crunching sounds as he shifted his weight and then planted his feet in the tub bottom and stood up. Glass fell from his shirt and jeans and he shook more loose. Brushing some out of his hair, he high-stepped out of the tub and into the bathroom.

Well, there was no way the Secret Plan was going to work as originally designed. Bubba was not supposed to see the clock was even gone... maybe not for days. But with his bathroom window pulverized in his bathtub there was very little chance that he would not notice his house had been violated. Maybe he'd just think it was a break-in, Huck thought. A burglar breaking in through the bathroom window, after clocks and stuff. God knew that Bubba didn't have much else that was worth stealing, except maybe Great-Grampa Puhzz's civil war sword. Heck, maybe there was a bright side to this bathroom window fiasco. Maybe he could grab the sword too.

Reassured, Huck tiptoed into the living room and up to the bookcase (it was a bookcase only in name, since Bubba's idea of a book was the latest issue of "Paint-Ball Battles Monthly.") Huck's breath caught as he saw it on the center shelf.

The clock sat in the center of the dim yellow haloes of light cast by Huck's flashlight. Slightly art deco in appearance, the layered wooden casing boasting a workmanship that is rarely seen anymore, it ticked quietly away, the famous ant riding the sweep second hand around and around through eternity. To Huck it was a thing of beauty.

He pulled a soft cloth sack from where he had tucked it on his belt and lifted the clock to put it inside. A cloud of dust arose and danced in the flashlight's beam and Huck quietly cursed his brother for letting the precious hair-loom fall into such a condition. It should be dusted regularly, he thought, maybe even polished with a little Pledge or furniture wax once a month. With the clock carefully stowed in the sack, Huck reached for the top of the bookshelf and pulled down the sword (knocking three empty coffee cans to the floor with a clatter.) He swung the scabbard over his shoulder. Then, unlocking the front door, he slipped out onto the porch. He had barely finished closing the door behind him when he heard a noise.

"Bubba F. Puhzz?" a voice called out in the darkness. The voice was smooth, rich, and familiar. There were also the sounds of footsteps, and then there was the snorfeling sound a dog makes when it snorts along the ground looking for a new place to pee.

"Horsefeathers!" Huck whispered.

Huck wasn't just using a quaint expletive when he said this. He was actually declaring the name of the individual who, with basset hound in tow, was approaching the Puhzz residence and cutting Huck off from his truck. He was trapped like a rat, stolen goods in hand, on Bubba's porch. In moments he would be discovered.

Big Doin's At The Chinese Baptist Church

"*There was just enough moonlight that he could make out the silhouette of the squat cabin that Bubba called home. During the day he could have seen the peeling paint and patch-up tarpaper that decorated its sides, but tonight it was just a black square against the sky.*"
    page 31

VI
The Wild and Untamed Emu
In which we are told the life story of Horsefeathers Snoqualmie and of Huck's one-time indiscretion

One wouldn't want to deviate too far from the exciting main narrative at this point but if the reader will excuse it, a small bit of background on the creature that is Horsefeathers Snoqualmie might be of interest. At least it might help spell out what Huck was up against in his current situation.

No one knows where the Snoqualmie family originally came from, but at some point early in the century they took possession of the Caretakers Cottage at the Sunset Memorial Cemetery. They weren't hired so much as they just moved in one day when the cottage was empty and the town fathers said, 'Well, okay, you can stay if you keep the cemetery up.' Harvey Snoqualmie, then the family patriarch, agreed to do so and thus started the Snoqualmie Family Funeral Home.

The Snoqualmie children never went to public school, as they were taught at home by their Momma, so nobody in town really knew the family all that well. Which, of course, helped perpetuate the notion that they were odd folk.

They seemed all the odder when Harper Snoqualmie bought the land next to the Cemetery in 1972 and started an emu ranch. There were other emu ranches in the mountains thereabouts, as well

Big Doin's At The Chinese Baptist Church

as a mink farm and two llama ranches, but the Snoqualmies practiced an unusual system whereby they let the emus out of their pens every afternoon for several hours of exercise. It was not unusual to see an emu or three nipping at the grass between the graves at Sunset Memorial or loping through a funeral service. (The local catholic priest, Thaddeus Mother, regularly stopped the ceremonies he presided over to yell "Get them ostriches outta here!" over and over until one of the Snoqualmies removed the offending birds.) After a few years the people of McKinleyville grew used to the birds and stopped complaining, especially once Heathcote Snoqualmie started selling huge green emu eggs for half the price of a dozen chicken eggs at his roadside stand. One emu egg made an omelet that would serve six. It was a definite bargain.

What really did the worst damage to the Snoqualmie family's reputation was that their Momma was a pretty lousy home-teacher. She didn't know how to add and thought that Australia and Ireland were both just south of Paris. Horsefeathers, the oldest girl, without any better instruction, had apparently learned to read from the headstones and monuments in the boneyard. One result of this was that she called everyone by their entire name ("Hello, Huckleberry Samuel Puhzz, how do you do?") and after memorizing the birthdate of every citizen of McKinleyville often added that to her greeting ("Hello, Huckleberry Samuel Puhzz, born January

Third Nineteen-hundred and fifty-six. How do you do?") It caused many people to give her a wide berth when she came into town, usually with one of her six basset hounds trailing on a leash behind her. It was a shame, really, because aside from the aforementioned conversational problems and a disturbing tendency to dress entirely in black she was a rather attractive woman.

In fact, one day just after he left High School, Huck had noticed Horsefeathers at the Food Mart. She'd been wearing a long black dress that stopped just above her ankles, which were covered in black fishnet stockings. The black pillbox hat with black lace that hung down almost like a short veil accentuated Horsefeathers' large doe eyes and white, pasty complexion. Something about the combination had aroused Huck's teenage libido, and he had approached her, regaling her with two stories of dreadful accidents at the mill and of his grandmother's lifetime search for more and better spoons.

The next day they met for lunch. Huck ran out of interesting stories (he only knew the three) but the normally quiet Horsefeathers just about burst her buttons. She talked a blue streak about the emus, about her Grandma Heloise' mysterious skin cream what had been stolen by the big soap company, and told Huck breathlessly the entire considerable history of the headstone, grave marker, and memorial manufacturing arts. Most of the girls Huck knew were snooty types that didn't give anybody but the

Big Doin's At The Chinese Baptist Church

quarterback the time of day, but Horsefeathers was different. She talked normal, he felt, almost like she was a guy. But one look at those fishnets peeking out from beneath her dress, caressing those magnificent ankles, and you knew that she wasn't a guy.

I won't say nothin' about the kiss, because gentlemen don't kiss and tell. But I'm telling you there was a kiss. We'll just leave it at that.

The whirlwind two-day romance of Huck Puhzz and Horsefeathers Snoqualmie came to a crashing halt later that afternoon when the infamous Hunsey Bourcarte spotted them as they left the Burger Barn. Still swelled up with manly pride and his new prominent position in town following the sinking of President McKinley in Old Man Frerichs' outhouse, Hunsey regularly took every opportunity to knock the blocks out from under those he considered inferior to himself (which, he figured, would prolong his own stay at the top.) Upon seeing Horsefeathers, Hunsey called out "Hey, ostrich-lovin' zombie girl!" and the quality of his insults degenerated from there.

Huck felt sorry for Horsefeathers, but his sensitivity to peer pressure doused those and any other feelings he had for her. He quickly joined Hunsey to go throw beer cans off the US 52 overpass at Humboldt Hill. What had he been thinking? No one in his or her right mind had ever dated a Snoqualmie. It just wasn't done.

In the years since their brief flirtation Huck

had thought about Horsefeathers only once in a blue moon, usually when he was watching a women's basketball game on ESPN at the Pump'n Munch or the documentary special "Necropolis: The World's Greatest Graveyards," which they showed twice a year on the local PBS station. And those times when he did think of her, well, sometimes for just an instant he would feel sad, thinking about what might have been.

It should be noted that Horsefeathers had two other characteristics important to Huck's current predicament on Bubba's dark porch. First, she hated trespassers, and it just so happened that Bubba's cabin adjoined both the cemetery and the Snoqualmie emu ranch. Second, she was a crack shot with the gun which even now was resting on her shoulder.

The way Huck saw it he had two choices. He could let Miss Snoqualmie catch him on Bubba's porch, fess up and expose his Secret Plan (probably losing the prized family hair-looms in the bargain), or he could start running like hell and take his chances that it was too dark even for a crack shot like Horsefeathers to hit him. Huck, still not a rocket scientist when considering these matters, chose the latter.

Running at full speed, a rather large antique wooden clock under one arm, a civil war sword under the other, and a switched-off flashlight between his teeth, Huck dashed down the hill across Bubba's back yard, cut across the corner of the cemetery, and

Big Doin's At The Chinese Baptist Church

scrambled up the gully to US 52. To his horror the snorfeling sound of Horsefeathers' basset hound was never far behind. As he reached the Highway he looked both ways in search of some refuge - some place to hide until she gave up. Where could he go that his infernal pursuer wouldn't follow?

The soft glow of a cross and two Chinese characters floating amidst the trees gave him his answer.

Huck scrambled across both lanes, along the highway shoulder and then cut up the side of the Church parking lot, pausing to hide behind a rusting Lincoln Continental parked at the front.

"Bubba F. Puhzz, is that you?" he heard a voice weakly call from the other side of the highway. "Listen, whoever's there! If you are trespassing on Puhzz or Snoqualmie family land, prepare to be ventilated!" Huck could hear a shuk-chik sound as she slid a shell into the chamber. The peril of the situation became clear to Huck. He was going to be shot dead by an old flame, carrying a clock and a hundred-and-fifty-year-old piece of cutlery.

Huck held his breath, trying to remain as quiet as possible. Then a miracle occurred. With a guttural "rump-rump-awk!" an emu burst out of the bushes at the edge of the cemetery and, bouncing on its three-toed feet, ran north toward the big marble piano that marked Royal "Four-Fingers" Cordova's burial site. Horsefeathers whipped around and watched the great bird do a lazy-eight around the

Madsen family and then disappear behind a mausoleum. The emu's sudden appearance and departure so perfectly distracted Horsefeathers that Huck couldn't believe his luck. If he had known how that very same emu would later reenter his life he might have reconsidered. But for now he felt lucky as hell.

Slowly the snorfeling sounds grew more distant and he saw the six-foot-four silhouette of Horsefeathers Snoqualmie against the purple sky, climbing the hill toward the cemetery. For a moment he imagined the strange, erotic combination of incongruous black fashions she might be wearing. But just for a moment. Really.

There wasn't time for more than that. He had a Secret Plan to complete. How was he going to get back to his truck without alerting her again? With a deep sigh Huck set the sword down on the tarmac and peered into the cloth sack at the clock. The top of each felt wet and he realized that he had been perspiring mightily during his flight across US 52. He pulled his shirttails out and wiped down the top of the clock and then along the sword's scabbard. It was as he performed this ritual that he became aware of the large number of cars parked in the church's lot.

Needless to say, Huck remembered his Neighborhood Watch training. Always notice the unusual. It is well known that no normal church has services on a Tuesday. Sundays, of course. The occasional Saturday. Sometimes a Wednesday-night prayer meeting. But Tuesday? It had to be some special Chinese thing, Huck figured, something called for in Mao's Little Red Book or spelled out in some saying of Confucius, or perhaps it was something even more sinister. For this was McKinleyville's one and only Chinese Baptist Church, and it was clear to anyone with two eyes that something big was going to happen tonight.

VII
Big Doin's At The Chinese Baptist Church
In which the titular Church finally makes an appearance in our story

Huck crawled carefully up to the large windows that filled the side walls of the Chinese Baptist Church. He had to see what the yellow devils were doing in church on a Tuesday night, the only night of the week that was, in Huck's mind, totally without any religious merit at all.

Not that all Asian-type people were yellow devils. Just the ones doing bad things in a church on Tuesday night. Huck was very proud of the fact that he did not have one racist bone in his body. In fact, in grade school he had even drunk out of the same milk carton as Chad Niger (pronounced like "tiger"), the only black student in his class. Huck didn't hold World War II or communism or that tank thing in

Tianenmen Square against everybody in town who happened to be of Asian descent. Every time he drove past the Chinese Baptist Church on Neighborhood Watch Huck always went out of his way to keep his eyes peeled for skulkers the same as he would for the Catholic church down the road, trying to be fair and all. Tonight was no different, and Huck went into Neighborhood Watch mode. No Christian Church had big doin's on a Tuesday night. He was sure that if he walked down to St. Josephus that the priest, Thaddeus Mother, would agree wholeheartedly. So, clearly, something was up.

Rising to his tip-toes, Huck realized that looking in the windows wasn't going to help, seeing as how they were made of stained glass. He could see a pretty picture of Jesus doing something, but not what was going on inside the church, so he took one glance back to his beloved hair-looms - to make sure they were still safe sitting there beside the rusting Lincoln Continental - and then he moved around toward the back of the church.

He stopped when he reached the corner of the building. From this vantage point a large U-Haul truck was visible (one with the state of Texas and a half-naked cheerleader painted on the side), pulled ass-end up to the church's back door. A plank ran from the truck bed down to the doorjamb, where a red and rust hand truck rested. A single word lit up in Huck's otherwise dim mind; contraband. The Chinese Baptists were smuggling contraband into the

Big Doin's At The Chinese Baptist Church

country with U-Haul trucks. Contraband was what smugglers were always smuggling when you heard about 'em on the TV. Huck wasn't exactly sure what contraband was, but he figured it had something to do with contras, and President Reagan had hated them like nobody's business, so it had to be bad news. With another furtive glance toward the precious clock he slipped around the corner, hopped the plank, and tiptoed into the church.

Huck wasn't sure what he had been expecting the inside of a Chinese Baptist Church to look like. Mostly he expected nail beds, hot bowls for branding pictures of dragons in your forearms like Chang Kwai Caine did in that old *Kung Fu* TV show, and lots of burning incense. Instead there were crosses, regular old pews, and a pulpit that would have turned Reverend Wheeler green with envy. Pretty clever, he thought, these smugglers disguising their Chinese Baptist Church as a regular church.

The sound of voices flowed from a large room to the right of the lobby. At first Huck thought they were speaking Chinese, but then he realized it was just a lot of voices speaking English, some of them laughing. Laughing in church! That proved right there that they weren't no ordinary Christians, Huck thought. He slid along the stained glass windows and took a peek inside.

The room off the lobby of the McKinleyville Chinese Baptist Church was filled with a kaleidoscope of color, but when Huck Puhzz stared into the room he missed almost all of it. He missed the big sign at the door that said in perfect English "Church Bingo & Casino Night." He missed the group of white-haired ladies in chairs with the smudged bingo cards. He missed the sight of Reverend Kim dealing cards at the "Poker For Flood Relief" table. He missed Mayor Fletcher (and her long-suffering husband who would rather have been at home building H-O trains) throwing dice at "Craps For Farm Aid." Huck didn't even notice the "Baccarat for Alcoholics Anonymous" booth. He stared right through the lemonade stand and the dreaded bake sale counter (which offered all the cakes that hadn't sold at the previous week's sale.) The sights and sounds of the busy room faded into the background of poor Huck's subconscious, and every ounce of Huck's attention became riveted on a single item.

The Red Cross Wheel Of Fortune sat to the right next to the emergency exit. Some ladies from the Centerton Non-Chinese Baptist Church had spent the better part of three weeks constructing the wheel for tonight's festivities. Betty Jean Essex had gone to a great deal of trouble to get real photo reference to make sure they got their Wheel Of Fortune accurate (at least, as accurate as it could be with the selection of paint colors they were offered at the Centerton Ace Hardware.) The letters and numbers were almost perfect, painted by Lolondra Hawks, who did the calligraphy for the Good Citizen Awards

Big Doin's At The Chinese Baptist Church

every summer. The Wheel was so perfect (at least from a distance) that Betty Jean had taped a paper-bag sign on the wall above it that said in bold laundry-marker letters "As Seen On TV."

Well, Huck's heart just about stopped.

Certainly, in some dark recess of his brain (and there were many) the mighty hair-loom ant was still ticking away madly, and still further down in the cracks and crevices a shiny civil war sword rested. But in the large vacant room at the top there was only the Wheel. Not just any wheel. But THE Wheel.

It was suddenly so three-dimensional. It was so big. The flippers made a snapping click-click-click-click-click as the spokes of the wheel rifled past them. Huck had always suspected that the Wheel was a TV trick, a computer image or a cartoon. But here it was, large as life, utterly complete except for the understandable absence of host Pat Sajak and the Queen of the Game Show. His fascination with the Wheel had been life-long, and no one else in the world could understand the intensity of it. The tight knot in Huck's stomach knew what was coming next before Huck's head did.

He had to have the Wheel.

Don't you see, it was just like the clock! These people couldn't really appreciate the wheel, at least not like Huck did. They just used it to raise money for some Chinese Baptist cause. They weren't capable of seeing the beauty inherent in the Wheel itself. If he'd understood the misguided medieval concept of the 'perfect solid,' Huck would have described the Wheel in just such a way. Of course he didn't, so he couldn't. But he felt it all the same.

I could describe the moment-by-moment events of the next two hours, but since they would bore you to distraction I will just say that Huck made his way back outside, checked on the clock and sword, and then made a daring dash across US 52 to rescue his truck. He was fairly sure he'd made it to the truck without attracting the attention of Horsefeathers Snoqualmie and her bloodthirsty basset hounds, although the intermittent snorfeling sounds he heard kept him on his toes. The truck started and he drove back across to the church parking lot, cleverly hiding the vehicle behind two oak trees and the back end of the rusted Lincoln Continental. He put the soft cloth bag containing the world's most amazing clock on the front passenger seat and the civil war sword on the front passenger floor. Then he sat there and waited for all the Chinese Baptists to go home.

People finally started to leave, a dribble at a time, around ten o'clock. Mayor Fletcher left with a great deal of fanfare (at least for McKinleyville) about ten-thirty. By eleven Betty Jean Essex and the Casino Night Planning Committee headed home for the evening news. Huck thanked God (appropriately) that church-going people also tended to turn in early. It was only eleven-fifteen when the remain-

Big Doin's At The Chinese Baptist Church

ing group of four people, which included Reverend Kim and three of his youngsters, started loading the Casino wares into the big Texas cheerleader U-Haul truck.

They were situating the Craps table in the truck when Huck sneaked past them into the church and found himself alone in the Casino room. He approached the Wheel with awe and stroked its side admiringly, thinking about the thousands of times he had watched its official Hollywood counterpart on TV. He almost fell into one of those Vanna White trances he got sometimes, but the sound of the Kims returning broke the spell. With superhuman strength he lifted the wheel, backed into the emergency exit doors, and threw them open. By the time the Kims arrived the door was closed and Huck Puhzz was gone, table and all.

As far as making it home clean after this point, I could say that only one hurdle still lay in Huck's path, but that would be a lie because there were several, and one was about to make its presence known.

With amazing agility that would have surprised his old boss at the mill (who, of course, thought Huck was still disabled with a back complaint), Huck carried the heavy Wheel across the parking lot and to his truck. As he got the edge of his prize up and onto the tailgate he heard a muffled hump-hump-hump and a swaying movement caught the corner of his eye. He balanced the Wheel on the tailgate edge and peered into the darkness.

There was an emu in the back of his truck.

The large, ugly flightless bird that sat in the bed, up against the cab, had been watching him while he wrestled with the great Wheel. Its beak curled upward like it was almost smiling at him. Huck looked both ways, expecting to see Horsefeathers and her rifle at any moment, but the erotic giantess was nowhere to be seen.

Huck gave the situation a bit of thought before proceeding (a highly unusual step.) He couldn't very well make a ruckus shooing the bird away, on account that it might alert the Chinese Baptists. It seemed his only choice was to load up the Wheel and deal with the emu later when he was safely away from the church.

The Wheel rolled into the truck bed, stopping inches short of the great pile of bird, and Huck closed the tailgate, jumped into the cab, and rolled out onto US 52 in neutral. He was halfway down the hill and already doing twenty miles an hour before he turned on the lights and started the engine. It came to life in a fitful rumble and the clutch popped into third gear.

As he tooled down US 52 toward home, Huck reflected on the night's activities. Amazingly, except for the feathered hitchhiker in the back of his truck, everything had turned out all right. He had possession of the clock, which had been the primary objective of his Secret Plan, but he also had Grandpa

Big Doin's At The Chinese Baptist Church

Puhzz's Civil War Sword and the amazing Wheel. Lady Luck had really been with him tonight, he figured. Hot damn, he was going to have to doublecheck those lottery tickets! That's what you got when you planned carefully. Creating a clever plan before you started something was the answer. There was absolutely nothing left to go wrong.

It was about this time that Bubba and his posse began to wonder why Huck hadn't arrived back with the whiskey.

VIII
Bubba's Posse On The Scent
In which everyone in Humboldt County heads for Huck's

Huck glanced back at the emu, which was smiling at him through the rear windshield. The bird's smug look as it stood unevenly on its knobby legs in the pickup bed made him consider taking a short side trip to Old Man Frerich's farm so that the cocky creature could take a swim in the outhouse with President McKinley, but he remembered that the precious Wheel was back there too, so he kept on track for home. No sense making silly mistakes when everything was going so well.

Unfortunately, if Huck hadn't been so busy thinking about Old Man Frerich's outhouse as he looked at the grinning emu in the rearview mirror, he might have noticed a tall, dark, lacey figure standing in the middle of the road about a quarter mile back, waving a rifle and a flashlight. But he was, so he didn't.

Bubba and the boys back at the Pump'n Munch had no way of knowing that, when he'd left them, Huck had snuck off to Bubba's place to steal a insect-infested clock and a bent civil war sword, and then had broken into the Chinese Baptist Church to take the congregation's Casino wheel, and then had gotten an emu trapped in the back of his truck as he carried the loot home to his trailer. They didn't even have a clue. As far as they were concerned, at least for the first hour or two, he'd gone down the block to the Safeway for a bottle of whiskey and the 'Express' line had been closed. By the third hour they were suspicious that he'd forgotten about them and gone home, which was okay except they'd been really looking forward to the whiskey. Bubba was particularly put out because it was his big party and he'd thought, at least for a few minutes, that Huck was really proud of him this time.

The posse was drowning their disappointment in beer when the door to the Pump'n Munch swung open and a large figure ducked through it. The giant's head barely cleared the door header and the butt of the rifle the giant carried thumped on the floor as it stopped just inside. Bubba, Big Kenny, Hampton, Sammy, Larry, and Little Larry all turned to face the intruder.

"Bubba F. Puhzz!" the giant declared, her long flowing tresses of jet black hair cascading out of a furry black cossack's hat. A heavy black denim duster covered her long, lacey black chenille dress, and her heavy black combat boots almost reached the dress. In between the dress and the boots the boys could spy an inch or so of black fishnet stockings that seemed painted onto her shapely ankles. Her ivory skin shone out of the surrounding darkness, her pale blue eyes the only color present from head to toe.

"Horsefeathers?" Bubba responded in a not-quite-drunk-but-hope-to-get-there haze.

"Somebody has broken into your house, Bubba F. Puhzz, through the bathroom window! And they have stolen one of my brother's, Harper H. Snoqualmie's, emus!" She banged the butt of her rifle on the floor again for good measure.

"What?" Bubba managed.

"Wake up, you drunken sot! You have been violated!" Horsefeathers yelled. Her words sunk in and Bubba's eyes grew big.

"Skulkers!" Hampton immediately deduced, because he was trained in the Neighborhood Watch arts as well. The posse stood as one, pushing their chairs back. Well, perhaps 'stood' is a strong word, since Big Kenny and Larry had noticeable wobbles, but the point is that they were no longer on their chairs and stools. Bubba grabbed the baseball bat he kept for beating off inexperienced robbers.

"Which way?!" he demanded.

Several miles away on US 52 a thought occurred to Huck as he drove home (which is notable in and of itself.) He realized that if he took the emu home it might serve as what they called "incriminating evidence" on Court TV or what they called a "smoking gun" when it involved any politician. Even Huck could figure out that when the sheriff found Bubba's bathroom window had been busted, the Wheel had been stolen from the Chinese Baptist Church, and an emu had gone missing - all on the same night and within four hundred yards of each other - he might put two and two together and deduce that the same person might be responsible for all three criminal acts. And if the emu were found munching on the grass in Huck's front yard it might look very bad for him. So the emu had to go. But he couldn't get the emu out of the truck until he'd got the Wheel out first, so he remained on a course for home, thinking about the best places one might dump an emu. All those nights of Neighborhood Watchin' and he ought to have seen at least one good emu dump site by now.

Huck's truck rumbled into his driveway and up to his trailer (finally waking Whizzer, who'd been asleep all day under the porch) about the same time that Bubba, the posse, and Horsefeathers stopped on US 52 directly between Bubba's cabin and the Chinese Baptist Church. They stopped because Rever-

Big Doin's At The Chinese Baptist Church

end Kim and the three second generation Kims flagged them down, yelling and hollering about how their church had been robbed. When Horsefeathers told Reverend Kim about the break-in at Bubba's house he became convinced that gangs (either the Bloods or the Crips, since they were the only gangs you ever saw on TV) or organized criminals (either the Mafia or the Yakuza, same notation) had arrived in McKinleyville. Billy Kim ran off to the Church with Little Larry to call the sheriff while Big Kenny, Hampton, and Bubba went up to the cabin to check out the damage and see what was missing. Reverend Kim, the other two Kims and Big Larry stood in the middle of the highway waiting for other cars to come by so that they could flag 'em down and tell 'em what had happened, since this was pretty big news in these parts. I don't rightly know what Horsefeathers was doing, so you'll have to make-believe that part for yourself.

Sheriff Freedom Kearney was in his office when Billy Kim's call was received. Sheriff Kearney had won his position in an election just two years before, beating the infamous Sheriff Danny Wadd (about whom it had been said that "the only thing redder than a Hawaiian sunset is the neck of Sheriff Danny Wadd.") I'd tell you the whole story of Freedom Kearney and how he beat ol' Sheriff Wadd, but it would slow down the pacing of our story and, besides, I gotta save something for the sequel. Suffice to say, Sheriff Kearney quickly put out the joint he had been gently nursing, hid it in the cigar tin at the back of his desk drawer, and dashed out to his cruiser to go investigate the heinous crimes that had been reported. His finely honed detective skills were already at work as he drove to the crime scene. A stolen sword. A stolen emu. A stolen Casino Prize Wheel. What was the connection? What was the "M.O."? (That was sheriff talk for "how the crook pulled it off." It's all very scientific.)

When he arrived the crowd in the middle of US 52 had grown. In addition to Bubba, Horsefeathers, the posse and the Kims, there was now an assortment of neighbors and motorists who'd been flagged down and told the story. Most of them parked in the Church lot and then joined the curious party on the highway. Just about everyone I've mentioned in this entire story was there, including Andy Petersen and Old Man Frerichs, who had been driving by and who was even older these days. Everybody was there with the exception of Huck (and Hunsey Bourcarte, who years before had moved on - but that again is another story.)

Before he got down to deducing, Sheriff Kearney exercised his powers for a few moments by waving his arms and saying "Move along, there's nothing here to see," and "Please stay back from the Crime Scene," even though the crowd was standing in the middle of the road and the crime scenes were back in the church and up at Bubba's. After he'd gotten everyone to move at least a foot or so from

Big Doin's At The Chinese Baptist Church

where they'd been previously standing the Sheriff whipped out his notebook and started asking questions.

The most important question, leveled at Horsefeathers (the only actual witness), was what kind of car or truck the "perp" (more sheriff talk) had been driving. She said she wasn't quite sure 'cause she hadn't seen it for all that long and it had been pretty dark at the time. But she thought it looked like a rusty red F-150 pick-up, the "Ford" name on the tailgate painted dirty white, with worn all-season mud & snow Generals on all four wheels, dents in the side, and an orange styrofoam ball stuck on top of the radio antenna. Oh, and there was a Casino Wheel and an emu in the truck bed.

The crowd became much quieter. The posse, in particular, came together around Sheriff Kearney and Horsefeathers. "Rusty red?" they asked. "An orange ball?" Hampton asked. "Slightly worn but good-traction steel-belted all-season mud & snow General 645s on all four wheels?" Sammy asked, because he worked at McKay & Sons, the local retail representatives of the General Tire Company. As Horsefeathers confirmed each question Bubba's alcohol buzz fell away a bit more until he stood there angry and, worse, sober.

"Huck," he said under his breath. Within moments the posse, the Sheriff, Horsefeathers, the Kims, and a great deal of the spectators were in their vehicles and headed down Highway 52.

IX
Our Conclusion
In which Huck pays for his crimes

It took a few minutes for Huck to wrestle the Casino Wheel up the stairs and into his trailer. He had to fold up his dining room table and put it in the shed in order to accommodate the Wheel, but that was perfectly fine with him. He got a couple of hooks from the kitchen drawer and hung the sword right above Grandma's spoon rack. And then he set the clock in its place, the altar of the Puhzz household, right on top of the TV.

The emu was still waiting out in the truck, licking under its wings doing something that Huck hoped wasn't too perverse. Emus were strange creatures. But he had to stop here for a moment to reflect on the glory of his success. He eased into his barcalounger, slowly raising the footrest and leaning back comfortably.

In front of him the view was breathtaking. The TV, which he'd turned on, displayed the latest episode of *Walker, Texas Ranger* ("wait, isn't that on Saturdays?" he thought for one split second before the view overcame him again.) On top of the TV sat the clock, the Eternal Ant sweeping around in concentric perfection. Higher still hung the spoons, the proud little shield reading "Little America" shining distinctively from amongst the "Columbuses" and "Terre Hautes" and "Visit Beautiful Grand Canyons."

Arching above the spoons was Great-Grandpa Puhzz's civil war sword, polished that very night in Huck's own sweat. And last, but not least, just to the right of the mighty altar, sat the Wheel, boldly decorated with its rainbow colors and dollar amounts.

It was Paradise.

Some people spend a lifetime trying to achieve this, he thought. They spent millions on shrinks and new age books and cruises with Kathie Lee Gifford. Most of 'em never found it. But he had. If he never experienced it again, at least this once he knew utter happiness.

He took a deep breath, letting himself settle in the cushions of the barcalounger, melting with satisfaction into the room. Yeah, he could get used to this. He wondered if, even as a child dreaming of Big Rock Candy Mountain and the Sea Of Chocolate, he'd ever imagined that such bliss was possible.

Huck might have gone on existing in his personal version of nirvana forever if the sound of a car engine, maybe two, and the rump-rump-awk of the emu in his truck hadn't brought him back to reality. He sat up in the barcalounger, kicking the footrest back into the chair with a snapping of misaligned armatures and springs. There were more engine sounds.

Peering out between the blinds of the living room's only window he could see cars up on the highway, moving very slowly. But there was movement in the woods between the highway and his trailer too, and he instinctively knew what it was.

"Skulkers!" he whispered, and he went to the closet for Grandma's shotgun. He also woke up Whizzer, who had fallen back to sleep lying up against the colorful Wheel. "We got skulkers!" he told the old hound, who acted as if he didn't really care. Still, Whizzer got up and stood next to his master. Hey, Whizzer wasn't a brilliant dog, but he knew who worked the can opener.

Slowly, carefully, Huck opened the front door and stepped out onto the porch, squinting into the dark. A car pulled up on the highway, then another, parking just south of his driveway. Their headlights went dark and then he couldn't see anything again. But although he couldn't see anyone he could still feel them skulkers, crawling around his woods. Four, maybe five carloads of 'em. There were twigs snapping in the darkness, leaves rustling from all sides. It was as if he were surrounded.

"Who's out there?" he yelled, raising the shotgun so that the villains could see he was capable of protecting himself. The emu let out another rump-rump-awk as if in answer.

"He's got a gun!" a voice yelled from halfway down the driveway. Scrambling sounds came from everywhere as the skulkers ducked for cover.

Then the world seemed to explode.

A bright spotlight suddenly blinded Huck, manipulated by hand from the door of Sheriff Kearney's black and white. Damn, Huck thought, if they can give the police lights that bright why can't they make a decent flashlight? A fusillade of lightbursts occurred as about a dozen cars' headlights came on, some pointed toward the trailer and some not. The yard was lit up like the middle of Yankee Stadium. Huck could see twenty or thirty people crouched in the bushes and Sheriff Kearney standing beside his patrol car. Bubba and the posse were right behind him (Bubba holding his baseball bat.) Most terrifying, Huck saw Old Man Frerichs standing behind a big oak on the side of the driveway.

Well, it weren't skulkers. No doubt about it, he was in the frying pan.

"Put the gun down!" the Sheriff said over his bullhorn in his most commanding voice (it really wasn't all that commanding, which was why he used his bullhorn at every opportunity.) "Put the gun down and come out of the trailer!"

Huck thought about this for a moment and then ducked back into the living room. This was too important a moment to turn over to his own bad judgment. He hadn't made a single good decision in his life and he probably wasn't going to start making them now. Feet dragging, Huck moved over to the great Wheel.

"Wheel of Fortune, please tell me what to do," he said, and then he gave the massive disc a mad yank, letting his fate spin with the Wheel. The flippers snapped on the pegs that bordered the Wheel's edge and then the click-click-click-click-clicks slowly diminished and it lost speed. Huck watched the space below the big red arrow with anticipation. With a soft bounce (that almost snapped the Wheel over to "Double Bonus Round") it settled on a space. Huck read the result aloud to Whizzer.

"Lose Your Turn."

Although Huck had never been "fast on his feet," he figured you couldn't very well argue with the Wheel Of Fortune. The jig was up. The coppers had caught up with him. And Vanna had spoken. Oh, he wasn't just going to give himself up and do hard time in the joint. No, he was going to negotiate. He had seen it a hundred times on *Law & Order* and *Court TV*. The accused gave up something, like a hostage, and then the D.A. gave him time off for good behavior or something like that. Huck figured a little horse trading might lower the heat.

"Take the emu!" he cried out, still ducking behind the trailer door.

"You're damn straight I'm taking the emu! Huckleberry Samuel Puhzz, what the hell has gotten into you?!" yelled Horsefeathers Snoqualmie from the bed of Huck's pickup truck, where she was cradling the wayward emu in her arms. To the right a figure stood up from behind the propane tank. It was Reverend Kim.

"We want our Wheel! We rent it from very expensive party place in Centerton! If it get back late you're paying the late fee, sonny! You got that?!" The Reverend fumed. Huck's stomach cramped at

Big Doin's At The Chinese Baptist Church

the thought of losing his beloved Wheel, but he realized that giving it up might be all that was standing between him and the Big House.

"Reverend, get back down! Huck, will you do me a favor and drop the damn gun?!" Sheriff Kearney bullhorned again. Well, those were all the cards he had to play. Tearing up a bit, Huck tossed Grandma's shotgun onto the porch and put his hands on top of his head, where his thumbs played in his not-quite-a-bald-spot.

"I ain't gonna shoot nobody!" he yelled back, and he carefully stepped down to the ground. He glanced back to see if loyal Whizzer had followed, but the hound had lain down underneath the barbeque and was asleep. "I give up."

Sheriff Kearney realized he wasn't going to get any more opportunities to use his bullhorn, so he tossed it in the back seat of his patrol car and walked up to meet Huck. He was shaking his head as they approached each other.

"Dammit, Huck! What the hell are you up to? This isn't like you! Breaking into your brother's house? Stealing the Chinese Baptist Church's Casino Wheel? Stealing Horsefeathers' emu? Are you on some of those extra-special pain killers?"

Well, Huck denied any drug use, but he admitted everything else, although his motives remained fuzzy in the lawman's mind. "Nobody else understands these things!" Huck tried to explain. "They're special! They're important!"

Luckily for Huck the posse pointed out that Huck had been drinking with them earlier. After Bubba quantified the amount of Black Velvet and beer that had been consumed the Sheriff was willing to write the whole thing off as a drunken binge.

When Sheriff Kearney consulted the injured parties Horsefeathers decided not to press charges (never underestimate the power of a kiss) and she scolded Huck a few times and then loaded up the emu in her truck and went home. The Sheriff was then able to talk Reverend Kim into doing the same (although it took some convincing) as long as Huck paid any late-return rental fees on the Casino Wheel. (These threatened "late fees" were, of course, a sham, since Reverend Kim hadn't rented the wheel at all. It had been painstakingly built, as noted earlier, by Betty Jean Essex and Lolondra Hawks.) The younger Kims hauled the Wheel out of the trailer and Big Kenny volunteered to drive it back to the Chinese Baptist Church in his truck. So, as far as plaintiffs went, that just left Bubba.

Bubba didn't look quite as forgiving.

"Are you pressing charges, Bubba?" the Sheriff asked. Bubba stared Huck straight in the eye. A long moment of silence ratcheted up the suspense.

"I don't figure I will," Bubba replied finally. "This is family, and we can deal with it inside of the family." The Sheriff nodded and rounded up the last of the gawkers and they all drove out one by one (although a few were disappointed there hadn't been

Big Doin's At The Chinese Baptist Church

any shooting, especially Old Man Frerichs.) That left just Bubba and the remains of his posse. "Wait here, boys," Bubba told them. "This is between me and Huck."

Huck wondered if he was about to get hit.

He gestured to the door, and the two of them climbed up the stairs and into the trailer. Huck thought about offering Bubba some whiskey, but then decided the timing would be poor. His brother just stared at him, as if he were waiting for something.

"I did it," Huck confessed.

"Yup," Bubba said, and he began to slowly pace around the tiny living room, stepping over the footstool and the dog (who had now moved inside to continue his 24-hour regimen of sleep.) Bubba stopped in front of the TV, where the clock sat and the spoons and sword hung in their places of honor. The eternal ant tick-tick-ticked around in front of him. Huck looked down at the floor.

"I'm sorry, Bubba, really I am. I just got kinda confused, that's all. I didn't mean to break your bathroom. There was just something inside that I had to have. I thought that it was more important to me than it was to anybody else... I guess that weren't very fair to you, huh?"

Bubba watched the ant go by for another few seconds and then reached up and lifted Grandpa Puhzz's civil war sword from the hooks upon which Huck had placed it.

"Well you can't have it," Bubba said. "You have to pay for your crimes and for taking what isn't yours. So I'm taking Grandpa's sword back home."

"But what about the - ?" Huck began.

"Don't argue. I'm taking Grandpa's sword back to my place," Bubba said, and he looked Huck straight in the eyes again. Then he stuck the scabbard under his arm and went out the front door, taking the steps careful-like. He shouted to the posse to head on back to the Pump'n Munch for more beers.

Huck watched Bubba's car disappear out onto US 52 and then he walked over to the TV and put his face right up against the glass of the hair-loom extraordinaire, following the ant on its endless procession around and around the numbered face. And Huck thought that maybe his brother deserved that promotion to night manager after all.

The Return Of The Teapot Dome

I

A Good Boy Gone Bad
In which Huckleberry Puhzz witnesses the worst side of human nature

At first it seemed like any other foggy McKinleyville March day to Huck Puhzz, just another weekly trip-to-town. The streets were grey, the buildings were grey, the city buses (so that they wouldn't look out of place) were grey, and, of course, the fog was grey.

Huck had started the day by picking up his mail. His mailbox out on Highway 52 had been washed into a culvert by the big El Niño storm, and he wasn't exactly known for being a handyman, so he had Jack at the post office hold his mail for him. He got it every other week when he came into town to pick up his disability check. After throwing away the mail, which was mostly bills, Huck had gone down the street and hung out with Billy Quick for a while at the Cigar-Store-Indian newsstand. They'd talked about how crazy that Saddam Hussein guy was and argued about whether the groundhog seeing his shadow meant more winter or less winter. Later on he'd bought a few tins of chew at the Safeway and then meandered down to where the Honda dealer was selling four-wheel off-road beach buggies by the dozen (even though the nearest beach you could legally ride them on was more than forty-six miles away.) Next he'd checked out the "miracle aisle" at the Bulk Foods Club to see if they had got any of those fifty-gallon drums of Dennisons' chili back in stock (one usually lasted Huck better than a month.) After that it was getting pretty late and if Huck didn't get home soon he'd miss his favorite TV show which, as you already know if you read the preceding story, was *Wheel Of Fortune*. So Huck hitched up his overalls and had just started back to his truck when he witnessed the first part of the crime.

This was an especially exciting moment for Huck. You see, Huck had never been "at the scene" in his life. Not once. He always saw the results of auto accidents from his truck window, creeping along at three-miles-an-hour and trapped in a line of rubberneckers after the ambulances had already taken all the cool bloody stuff. He always saw the black smoke billowing up into the sky from six blocks away and when he got to its origin point the firemen had just doused the very last flames. And as for crimes taking place, well, those had always been restricted to television, radio, newspapers, and wild gossip. He'd never seen one in action "at the scene." Huck figured he was cursed to always be just a few minutes behind all the excitement. But his luck was changing.

When he thought about the event later, Huck

The Return Of The Teapot Dome

remembered it all as having happened in slow motion, like those reenactments on *America's Most Wanted* or like when the Six Million Dollar Man did just about anything. A teenager came burstin' out of J.J.'s Bookstore with a stack of books in his arms heavy enough that Arnold Schwarzenegger would have had a tough time bench pressing 'em. An employee of J.J.'s Bookstore, poor ex-Bookarama clerk Keith (whose long and tragic story will be saved for the next book) came running out onto Fifth Street screeching and hollering "Thief! Shoplifter!" In a flat second the criminal had dashed around the corner and up the alley between the Korean Food Market and the Junk Garden Antique Boutique.

Now, from Huck's standpoint at the streetcorner he could see what the screaming clerk couldn't; the perpetrator dumping the load of literature into the back of a dark blue Chevy and then leaping into the driver's seat.

For a minute Huck's lizard brain tried to make a decision concerning what to do. A hundred questions raced through his mind. Should he chase after the criminal? Should he inform Poor Keith, the screaming clerk, of the ne'er-do-well's location? Should he scream a bit himself? Should he holler for the Sheriff? Would the Sheriff hear him? How far was he from the Sheriff's office? What sorta books do you suppose are worth stealing? Why not rob a bank or liquor store like any other self-respecting criminal? Well, before Huck had a chance to decide a course of action (mercifully enough) the Chevy started and then roared up the alley onto Third Street and out of sight. Poor Keith ran up to Huck's side.

"Did you see where he went?" the clerk asked breathlessly.

"Thataway," Huck told him. You know, he'd always wanted to say that.

This single exciting event would have been enough to provide Huck with six month's worth of conversation all by itself, maybe a year's. In fact, he was so anxious to get down to the Pump'n Munch Gasoline & Convenience Center to tell Bubba[1] all about the day's excitement that he almost left his house trailer before Vanna White waved goodnight. Huck had no idea that the day, improbable as it might seem, had one more related adventure to offer.

It was already dark out, which meant that Bubba's posse would be crowded around the donut bar or the snackin' tables, drinking free beer and forcing their opinions on each other, so Huck knew he'd have a sizable audience to regale with the afternoon's story.

Sure enough, when Huck entered he saw that Big Kenny (who had recently slimmed down to a svelte 360 pounds) was parked at the Ms. Pac-Man machine with a roll of quarters. Hampton and Sammy sat at his shoulder waiting for their turns.

---

[1] *Bubba Puhzz, Huck's brother and the establishment's esteemed night manager. If you need to know this, go back and read the first story again.*

Larry and his son Little Larry were at the donut counter with Bubba having a complex political discussion. Well, actually they were just complaining about how the Centerton Garbage Company had bribed the city council in order to beat out Summerville Disposal for the local garbage contract. "There's more money to be made in garbage than in any other industry in this county," Little Larry was saying, and as far as the posse was concerned, truer words were never spoken. There was a series of blooping whines as Ms. Pac-Man successfully ate three evil ghosts in succession.

"They're all crooks," Larry said. "All politicians start as real estate agents or lawyers. Either way, they've already had to ditch their morals on account of their jobs. Come next month I'm not gonna vote for a one of 'em." Bubba nodded sagely as if he was paying attention, but secretly he was praying that Huck intended to change the subject. Or at least bring in some more beers from the freezer in the alley.

"I was at the scene today, boys, of a most spectacular crime," Huck began.

"Hold that thought," Bubba said. "Can you pop out to the freezer and grab the two six-packs of Mickey's in the ice tray?" Big Kenny paused at the videogame console and everyone in the room looked beseechingly at Huck, who shrugged and headed for the screen door that opened onto the alley.

And that, as they say, was serendipity.

Huck stopped short at the freezer when he heard voices in the alley. Two years of serving the Neighborhood Watch every Saturday night, driving up and down Highway 52 looking for society's reprobates with nothing but beer for company, had honed Huck's steely instincts for observation to a fine edge. This wealth of experience spoke to him now, and he knew without a shadow of a doubt that the two individuals talking quietly in the alley behind the Pump'n Munch were grade-A up-to-no-good skulkers.

Tiptoe-ing on injun feet, Huck sidled up to the freezer and peeked around the rusty hinges to get a good look. There were two of them, an older guy who looked like Willie Nelson but without the bandana around his head, and a teenager who looked vaguely familiar to Huck.

"I thought you didn't have any money," the Willie Nelson guy said, taking a wad of bills from the teenager.

"I sold some books," the kid said.

"That was smart," the singer's doppelganger replied, and he handed the teenager a baggie filled with a green leafy substance. The country-music clone moved off down the alley and the teenager walked briskly to the dark blue Chevy in the parking lot, started it and drove off. But not before his face was well lit for just an instant beneath the gas pump lights of the Pump'n Munch.

Huck's head became light and then the few

wheels inside it that were still in operation started turning. The skulker was a user of illicit substances. The skulker was the exact same criminal what had stolen that titanic stack of books from J.J.'s that very afternoon. And, most amazingly, the skulker was Victor Fletcher, son of the mayor of the great town of McKinleyville.

II
Politics Is As Politics Does
In which the big campaign begins

After Huck brought Bubba and his posse the two six-packs of Mickey's that had been stowed in the Pump'n Munch's alley freezer he went straight home. He didn't tell the boys about the spectacular crime of thievery that he'd witnessed that afternoon. He didn't tell them about the depraved crime of narcotic sales that he'd witnessed just moments before behind the Pump'n Munch. And he didn't tell them that he'd recognized the person who had been the perpetrator in both cases. The identity of this particular criminal changed the rules as far as Huck was concerned. The guilty party had been none other than Victor Fletcher, former high school football quarterback, former winner of the 1992 County Science Fair, and son of the mayor of the great town of McKinleyville.

Now, you may think I'm about to launch into the colorful and amazing story of Victor Fletcher and how he dropped like Icarus from the heights of football stardom and academic excellence to the ignominy of shoplifting and casual drug use. But I'm not. Firstly, because Victor's tale was rather typical for any average teenage American White Anglo-Saxon Protestant in the latter half of the twentieth century who grew up with indulgent, upper-middle-class absentee parents who never gave their children a strong moral compass. And secondly, because this story is about Huck.

The fact is that Lady Luck had been working the opposite side of the street from Huck for quite a while now and therefore any time something of import happened he tried to analyze it, first and foremost, as an opportunity. He was in possession of very specialized knowledge, and before he started sharing that knowledge with every Tom, Dick, and Bubba down at the Pump'n Munch he was going to have to consider his options. You just didn't get anywhere in life without considering your options.

Huck rolled down the windows in the truck as he drove home and let the cold night air hit him square in the face (along with a couple of bugs.) One by one he checked off the possibilities.

The most obvious course of action was that he could report the crimes to Sheriff Kearney and be done with it, but there was no opportunity in that. A devious mind might consider blackmailing the mayor with the information, but before you start going down that road let me tell you that Huck was an honest man and didn't think about it more than once... or twice. Nope, he was raised by his Grandma with the Good Book in her right hand and a manzanita switch in the other, and he wasn't about to sully her memory by becoming a blackmailer. So just how, exactly, was he going to find his opportunity?

It was late when he pulled up behind his trailer, almost running over old Whizzer as he did, and he and the hound dog took the stairs one at a time and then collapsed in the living room (Whizzer on the floor, Huck in the barcalounger.) He flipped on the TV, but even though one of his favorite episodes of *Hogan's Heroes* was on he wasn't really paying attention. His mind was still turning over the possibilities and getting, frankly, nowhere.

Much later, Huck was dozing (actually, he was alternating snores with Whizzer) when the Late Movie ended and the television station announced it was signing off for the day. A faded, scratched, and dirty film came on showing the Washington Monument and Capitol Building, and the White House from Pennsylvania Avenue (which was inhabited by two Edsels and a line of spectacularly finned gas-guzzlers.) The first monaural notes warbled from the television set and a soprano who was probably dead by now started belting out the Star Spangled Banner.

Huck's eyes popped open and he stared, hypnotized by the pink-and-gray flag that flapped above the Jefferson Memorial. "...what so proudly we hailed..."

In that moment Huck knew exactly what he had to do.

Everyone has a dream. Even Huck Puhzz had a Dream.

Huck's Dream had started to coalesce when he was about eleven years old. Ever since that time it had hovered there in his subconscious. On the rare occasions he thought about it, lying in bed at night and staring at the ceiling when it was too hot to sleep, he would assure himself that - when he grew up - he would certainly fulfill his Dream.

Of course, by the age of forty-two most people would already consider themselves "all grown up," but to Huck "grown up" was always a place just over the horizon, just a few more days beyond the twilight of youth he was still enjoying. "Grown up" was when you were gray and bald and hated rock & roll. Although Huck's hair was graying at the temples, and admittedly it was thinning slightly at the crown, he still very clearly loved rock & roll. And country & western for that matter. Course, he couldn't stand none of that rap stuff because that was for people who were members of gangs and lived in the big city. But that still didn't mean you were "grown up."

Now, listening to a forty-year-old recording

of the National Anthem, it came roaring to the fore with a vengeance. The Dream.

The Dream was not "The American Dream" (a designation that smacks of provincialism anyway) and "The Dream" was more than just Huck's simple expression for achieving something more in life. To anyone else (say, you or I) The Dream might be considered our lifeplan, our goals, the direction in which we wanted our lives to move. But no one Huck knew had ever had a lifeplan, a direction, or a goal any more complex than getting tanked next Saturday night at The Fifty Yard Line on H Street while watching the ESPN NFL game on the big screen. So to Huck the concept of his personal Dream implied more than just a series of goals to be achieved. It implied that, among the mundanes who shared beer with him at the Pump'n Munch and who would probably still be there eating day-old donuts and slamming Bud Lite when they were crowding seventy, he alone had a destiny.

It was the autumn of 1967 when Huck's destiny, in the form of The Dream, first suggested itself to him through the most unlikely of sources; a book.

At first young Huck had faced the book report which his teacher, Miss Gilbert, had assigned him with dread, seeing as how he'd never really been admired by anyone for his reading skills. Wicked teacher that she was, Miss Gilbert had limited the selection of books he could choose from, which right away eliminated *Spider-Man, The Incredible Hulk,* and

Sugar & Spike. No, she wanted him to choose from *My Friend Flicka, Brighty Of Grand Canyon, The Black Stallion,* and a bunch of other horse and mule books that were mostly for girls. Only after an hour of staring at the book spines and wishing he were out playing with his matchbox cars did Huck spy the book that would change his life.

In silvery letters on a black spine he read the title; *Augustus Caesar's World* by Genevieve Foster (published by Charles Scribner's Sons, New York, copyright 1947 if you really must know.)

It wasn't so much the story of the Emperor and his rule over ancient Rome that captivated Huck. And although he identified somewhat with young Octavius, the teen who would be Augustus, and his Hardy Boys-like adventures with his pal Agrippa, that really wasn't what fascinated him either. In fact, Huck didn't have the slightest idea why he skulked in and lifted the book from the school library and then hid it under his bed where his mother wouldn't find it. Now, thirty years later, it was still one of only three books Huck owned.

Huck could still remember - if he tried - the day he started reading the book. He and Hunsey Bourcarte had climbed up to the top of Kneeland Hill to shoot off bottle-rockets and illegal fireworks and smoke cigarettes Hunsey had stolen from his dad. They had just set off four sets of fireworks underneath some poor farmer's cow (probably the same one they'd tipped over the week before) and Hunsey had gone chasing after the cow to see how big its eyes had gotten. Huck stayed where he was, though. From the top of the Kneeland heights you could see all the way from McKinleyville to Centerton, across Humboldt Bay and over the spits to the Pacific Ocean itself. There in the warm breeze, sitting in the moist grass, he'd read the adventures of two young scalawags, Octavius and Agrippa. Not so unlike Hunsey and himself, they spent their summer days visiting soothsayers and running on the hills of Apollonia (which Huck supposed was very far away from Humboldt County.) If he closed his eyes and thought hard he could still see the pages of the book fluttering in the wind, feel the warm breeze on his face, and hear the screech as Hunsey set off another volley at the cow.

Later that afternoon they stole Hunsey's mom's sheets and, draping them around their bodies like togas, they had played "Roman Senate" and taken turns betraying each other and stabbing each other in the back.

Huck had gotten a C- on his book report and damn if it wasn't the best grade he ever received (probably because it was the first time he'd actually read the book he was reporting on). Momma threw him a pizza party with balloons for getting such a good grade. Bubba really hated that, because he'd gotten a C+ in PE just the quarter before and hadn't gotten a pizza party. Of course, the bar was set a bit higher for Bubba. Not much higher. Barely higher. But higher. Momma pretty much went and ruined the point of the evening later, though, when she took Huck to the front of the refrigerator, where the golden report was attached with a magnet advertising the Barnes Collectible Spoon Company, and said, "Take a good long look at it, boy. Your crowning glory. Soak it up. This is your moment in the sun. It's all downhill from here." Don't blame her, though. Momma had already sampled a couple of tequila shooters.

Well, once the report was turned in and the pizza party finished Huck promptly forgot it and the book as well. It wasn't until fifteen years later, when he finally moved out of Momma's house and into his trailer, that he found the dusty volume still under his bed. He almost threw it away. But despite the intervening years of vacuum, something had stuck in the back of his mind. Something about how some regular kid named Octavius could grow to become Augustus, emperor of the entire world. That was it — Huck had begun to actually believe, way down deep in the animal recesses of his mind, that despite his simple origins and simple education he still had a shot at greatness. That belief, that he was destined for something greater, became The Dream.

Of course, once he stuck the book away on a shelf in his trailer and went back to work he promptly forgot The Dream too. Every now and then it would raise its ugly head and make him feel guilty about his currently aimless and pointless life, but a few

The Return Of The Teapot Dome

hours of TV usually sucked it back into oblivion. Those who can, do. Those who can't just avoid thinking about it.

But here and now he could think of nothing but The Dream, and his course of action was crystal clear.

Bubba thought that Huck was nuts.

"You're gonna what?" Bubba asked him. Of course, Huck hadn't expected much support from his brother considering their well-known sibling rivalry. But at least he figured Bubba would take him seriously.

"I'm gonna run for mayor," he said. It was an elegant solution. If he ran for office against Mayor Fletcher she couldn't say one bad word against him, on account of how he was keeping mum about what a skulker her son was. In fact, she'd have to say nice things about him. He'd get swept into office and then he'd be making the really big bucks. He knew that much, because Lolondra Hawks worked for the city as an accountant, and she'd told him that she made the big bucks. If she could make big bucks in that kind of menial no-good job then the mayor, Huck figured, must be pulling down fiscal manna from heaven. It was so simple he couldn't understand why it hadn't occurred to him right away.

"Don't you gotta register with some secretary or something to run for mayor? Or get some signatures from people going in and out of the Post Office?" Hampton asked from the snack table where he was pulling the embroidery out of the store's baseball caps string by string.

"You don't got a First Lady," Big Kenny pointed out. "I think you gotta have a First Lady. Maybe you could ask Horsefeathers Snoqualmie. I hear she's still sweet on you." Huck turned red.

"Mayor Fletcher hasn't got a First Lady," Hampton said. "Is her husband a First Man?"

"First Gentleman," Sammy corrected.

"I think you gotta be a lawyer or a real estate agent before you can run," Larry said, shaking his head with disgust. "But if you don't, wouldn't that just flip the bird to 'em all if you won?"

"It would. It surely would. So, you want to be my campaign manager?" Huck asked him. Larry sat, thought, and chewed for a minute, and then he agreed.

And that is how it happened. Huck immediately marched down to City Hall. The McKinleyville government complex, which included City Hall, a county jail, a county courthouse, and the public library (conveniently tucked directly underneath the jail) was a suite of six adjoining buildings with wildly different architectural styles, built by six different architects and constructed with six different federal grants. California Magazine had awarded the resulting pile the dubious honor of being the ugliest city block in the state. The County Board Of Supervisors was negotiating for yet another grant and talk-

The Return Of The Teapot Dome

ing to yet another architect in order to build a seventh ugly building in the spot currently occupied by the parking lot.

Inside the ugliest of the existing six, Huck inquired of city secretary Betty Bellar about how, just exactly, a person went about running for the position of mayor of McKinleyville? To her credit, Betty kept a straight face and provided Huck with a stack of election forms, assorted rules and regulations, and several flyers for the 4-H's Sunday Pancake Feed.

Still, there was just one touchy part necessary to get the whole ball rolling.

Besides filling out the dozens of forms, Huck knew, he would also have to make his pitch to Mayor Fletcher. After all, that was the genesis of this little exercise. He had to let her know that he knew what a skulker Victor was, and that he had the goods on him. And, more importantly, he had to tell her what the price of his silence was; that her campaign would have to treat his campaign with kid gloves throughout the election, even though he would be free to participate in all of the traditional American mudslinging, accusations, and demeaning physical descriptions.

So how was he to tell her?

If he told her directly to her face, Huck figured, it might be considered ungentlemanly, and besides, he might possibly get hit. So instead he got out a piece of paper (actually, he used the back of one of the Pancake Feed flyers) and wrote a short, formal note:

>Dear Mayor Fletcher,
>   I know that your son is a skulker and criminal deviant. I saw him steal the books from the bookstore and saw him buy illegal drugs from a guy whom looked like Willie Nelson behind the Pump'n Munch. I will look the other way if you keep your trap shut when I run against you to be the new mayor.
>   Have a nice day,
>   Your opponent

Huck thought that signing it "your opponent" was an incredibly brilliant stroke, since anonymity would force Mayor Fletcher to be nice to everyone else running for mayor and, of course, it would cover his behind if Sheriff Kearney took a dim view of the whole thing. Huck held the note up in the brown light that struggled through the dirty window above his kitchen sink and smiled. The crowds in the forum cheered and the criers on the Seven Hills spread the news as parades of elephants marched up the Via Sacra. At last, Huck Puhzz was about to fulfill his imperial destiny.

III
Tales From The Mighty Groove Of The Last Rainbow Commune
In which Heavy Metal, Buddhism, and Islam give way to the spiritual power of television

Huck Puhzz was not the first person in McKinleyville, of course, to attempt to rise from obscurity to the heights of elected public office. In fact, a person of prominence already described in these tales arrived in Humboldt County a penniless hitchhiker.

Back then this indigent teenager went by the name Harold. But when he arrived in Humboldt County to attend the State University in Centerton he started going by the name Led (which he'd always believed was Mr. Zeppelin's first name). Led always hated school. Math was too hard with all of its laws and formulas, and even in English, where he sometimes wrote stories, the teachers constantly tried to impose order in the form of grammar, spelling, and punctuation. Only now in college, when he was introduced to Chaos Theory, did he find a scholarly subject he could identify with.

Outside of the obligations of school Led's life was his guitar and his music. He spent his nights and weekends thrashing and smashing to the point where his hearing was often a tad less efficient than his grandmother's. He loved the chaos in the sounds he created, the dissonance when he banged on the electric guitar strings with a spoon. It somehow meant something.

The music was also his escape from life, because after twenty years none of the adults in his life - the parents, guardians, teachers, community leaders, politicians, doctors, friendly store clerks - not one of them - had ever answered the question that he most wanted answered. "WHY?" It wasn't the most complex of philosophical questions, but then Led wasn't the most complex of teens.

The question was partly answered, at least, when Happy Today, Grand Father and nominal leader of the Last Rainbow Commune entered his life. The Commune was nested in the redwoods above the sleepy forest town of Garberville, just a spit and a holler south of McKinleyville. If you ever wondered what happened to all the hippies after 1967 (not counting the ones who cut their hair, put on suits and got MBAs), well, this is where they ended up, striving to keep the dreams and ideals of the Summer Of Love alive. Over the years the town had been officially proclaimed a haven for draft-dodgers, a nuclear-free zone, and by town ordinance it was illegal to smoke anywhere, even outside (well, tobacco anyway.) For many it was a little slice of heaven. Personally, the only reason Led had joined the commune was because the rent was so cheap.

But once there Led definitely appreciated Happy's Primary Message, the one Happy shared with The Family at every meal, the one that was written on posters hanging in every room; "The point of life, dear friends," he would say, "is to be happy every single day of your life and try to make the others around you happy. And to never infringe on another's happiness." Well, that sort of made sense. A talk he had with Happy one night around a Last Rainbow bon fire that stuck with him slightly longer;

"Why else live than to be happy?" Happy asked him. "Once upon a time this whole planet was nothing but hydrogen atoms. Little, tiny one-proton atoms. Now we are these incredibly complex living organisms. But for all that complexity we still all die. In two hundred years no one will remember we ever existed. Eventually the sun will expand as it depletes the gases that let it shine and, in those final stages, it will engulf the Earth and burn it into a cinder. The sun will absorb the Earth and everything on it, including every atom that is now a part of your body. Then it will be cast out as denser metals, which will someday come together in a nebula to form a new star, around which new life might arise."

"You mean," he'd asked incredulously, "my body will become heavy metal?!"

Well, that wasn't exactly the message Happy was trying to share, but it worked for Led so Happy just said, "Oh, yes. Heavy heavy."

In the days that followed that particular revelation Led changed his name to Cosmos, and began his own church, the Church Of The Hydrogen Atom, a sect which lasted all of six months. But before too long he realized that he was still lost, drifting through classes, living his life without order or purpose.

When he met Lotus, a really cute girl who lived at the commune and was studying architecture at the college, he converted to Buddhism and changed his name to Siddhartha. This transformation lasted three weeks (about the same length of time it took him to realize that Lotus wasn't going to sleep with him.) He converted to Islam and changed his name to Mohammed during the Gulf War. Then he impulsively changed his name to Freedom and became a full-time volunteer for Amnesty International, dropping all of his classes and walking the streets of Garberville in handcuffs to protest political prisoners everywhere. This transformation stretched on for six whole days.

Finally, one April night, he got exceptionally stoned and turned on the television.

And Charlton Heston filled the screen. Clad in robes and sporting a long white beard, Heston-as-Moses stood atop a mountain and spoke to God, getting holy advice, divine pointers, and spiritual recommendations. Freedom was transfixed.

Two nights later, even more stoned, he flipped on the television.

And Charlton Heston filled the screen. Heston-as-John The Baptist stood hip-deep in the River Jordan dunking Hollywood extras to aid in their salvation. Freedom's breath was taken away.

Was there some sort of cosmic message here, addressed to him?

The next night he deliberately got stoned just in time for the six o'clock movie.

And Charlton Heston filled the screen. This time Heston-as-Ben-Hur knelt before Jesus Christ and offered him a glass of Seven-Up or something. But the religious details weren't important to Freedom.

You see, even if you had pointed out to Freedom that these films were part of a biblical epic film festival that KIEM-TV was showing because it was Easter week... well, he just would have told you that it was all part of the cosmic plan. He'd become convinced that these images were on the television for him and him alone. Of course, Freedom was interpreting them in his own unique way. No, it wasn't any holy message derived from these films' religious themes that spoke to his soul. No, it wasn't the Commandments or Christ's teachings to Ben-Hur that reverberated in his mind. Not a word of them. Instead, it was the strong chin and bass voice of the man, Charlton Heston himself. You see, Freedom had decided that Charlton Heston was his own personal spiritual guardian.

The entire series of events might have faded away in a few weeks like all of his other 'conversions,' except for what happened the next night when he got really ripped and warmed up the tube.

Once again Charlton Heston filled the screen. But this time the great man was wearing blue jeans and a khaki shirt and had a really big rifle slung over his shoulder. Standing next to him was a man in a gray uniform. The letters at the bottom of the screen identified the uniformed man as Oklahoma County Sheriff's Deputy Dick Wells. "Not every law enforcement officer wants to take away your guns," Sheriff's Deputy Dick Wells was saying. "We're here to protect you, but you can help by protecting yourself."

"We need more dedicated men like Sheriff's Deputy Dick Wells," Charlton Heston said, his mighty jaw muscles flexing as his noble voice caressed each word. The screen faded to a bright symbol with the letters NRA in its center. Then it was over. A hush fell over the room.

"We need more dedicated men like Sheriff's Deputy Dick Wells," Freedom repeated, as if in a trance. And there began what became known in the halls of the Last Rainbow Commune as his HestonQuest. By week's end Freedom had enrolled in the Community College's law enforcement program and police academy. Just twenty brief months later Freedom Kearney became a deputy sheriff in Humboldt County.

And that was the conclusion of Sheriff Kearney's spiritual journey. Ever since then he's been working hard, protecting the people of Humboldt County. I suppose I could tell you exactly how he beat old Sheriff Wadd in the election, but there's not much to say. After a few years Freedom became a senior deputy, and with the backing of Garberville and all his old friends at the Last Rainbow Commune he decided to run in the next election against the tyrannical incumbent Sheriff. That man, Sheriff Danny Wadd, just two months before the election was involved in a minor hit-and-run and he tried to pay off his poker pal, the Publisher of the Centerton Post-Standard, to keep it out of the news. As always happens, the news got out anyway. (The news editor at KIEM-TV was a woman and therefore was never invited to play in the guys' poker game. Tough luck for old Sheriff Wadd.) The public got angry and Freedom ended up winning the election by default. Isn't that the way it always is with politicians? They never get in trouble for the things they do, just for trying to cover them up.

As for Sheriff Freedom Kearney's spiritual quest, he's a happy man today. And in his office, right above the American flag, hangs an autographed picture of Charlton Heston.

IV
McKinleyville's Foremost Man Of Letters
In which we meet Bob Thalia and his muse

Any day of the year (Christmas and Thanksgiving included) if you were to stop by the Eureka!-I-Found-It Coffee Shop in downtown McKinleyville after midnight you can get a chance to view, first-hand, the town's foremost man of letters. The coffee shop's decor and menu can't compare to the fancy Happy Kup franchisee over in Centerton, but as run by Denise, her husband Art and their daughters Laura and Jean, it is a family sort of eating establishment and that has always suited the town's eminent writer just fine. Plus, this was the only place in town where his muse would speak to him.

Bob's muse was Buster K. Melpoman... Melpomein... Melpomene... well, no one quite knew the proper spelling or pronunciation, but Buster always sat at the bar in the Eureka!, four stools from the end in front of the pie cabinet, from midnight until three a.m. Buster was "fond of the vine," as Denise used to say, which really meant that Buster was a wino and was sloshed about twenty-four hours a day. Every night around eleven-fifty Buster would stumble into the Eureka, say hello to Veronica the Night Manager in breath that could power most small camp stoves, and plant himself on his stool.

No one knew Buster's history - when he'd come to McKinleyville or what had happened in his youth that drove him into the bottle. Most folk were pretty sure that throughout most of the year he lived in a cardboard box in the alley behind the Sea Shanty (McKinleyville's secret seafood answer to Centerton's Neptune's Delight, an overpriced tourist trap). When pressed to guess they figured that he was around fifty years of age (although the street always added about ten years, kinda like how TV always adds ten pounds.) And, lastly, they were absolutely positive that Buster liked to talk to himself.

When Buster first started coming into the Eureka!, babbling and accusing the empty air around him of a variety of sins, Veronica regularly called Sheriff Wadd. The no-nonsense lawman (a kind description) would come, knock Buster around the ears a few times, and then haul him off to the drunk tank for a sleepover. After a while the regulars got tired of the ruckus that Sheriff Wadd made and got used to Buster, preferring his tirades to the Sheriff's. They even managed to overlook the improper and obscene words in Buster's rants, which were colorful and frequent. So Veronica took her cue from the customers and just let him be.

Well, early that fall Bob Thalia, who at the time wrote the McKinleyville beat for the Centerton Post-Standard, started coming in late on Tuesdays and Thursdays. Being a newspaperman, Bob was used to listening to people carefully for his stories, and for the first time someone actually listened to what Buster was saying.

Veronica thought Bob was out of his can when he started in one night writing down the nonsense that Buster was spewing.

"Do you hear what he's saying?" Bob asked her.

"Nah, I just tune it out. You gotta tune it out, or you'll go as crazy as he is," she explained, but

Bob only had ears for Buster. He took down each and every word the homeless man said, and when Buster sauntered out around three a.m. to find his box Bob gathered up his yellow legal pad and hurried home to type the whole thing up on his word-processor-thingy.

This dictate-and-transcribe process went on for some time, but to cut to the chase Bob submitted some of these writings to different magazines... oh, The New Yorker, Utne Reader, National Review Of Poetry, and a few dozen artsy-fartsy literary rags. Lo and behold, some of 'em started getting published. J.J.'s bookstore made sure they double-stocked any issue of a magazine or newspaper with a piece written by homeboy Bob Thalia. The townfolk were especially proud of him since Centerton didn't have a nationally published author of their own.

After the first piece, "FBI Spies In My Pants," appeared in New World Quarterly, Bob arrived at the Eureka! each and every night to meet Buster. When the royalties started to come in Bob started buying Buster a square meal every night, and while Buster ate and talked Bob wrote it all down. About six months after the first piece was published Bob signed with a newspaper syndicate for his own daily column called "The Screed," ostensibly written by "Robert M. Thalia," but in fact dictated to him nightly by one Buster K. Whatever.

The reviews were amazing.

"The collective resentment of the American

The Return Of The Teapot Dome

people toward the governmental and corporate bureaucracy following the collapsing promise of the mechanical, industrial and silicon ages is distilled in Thalia's hands into tiny chunks of devastatingly acid text, dropping like napalm on the reader and then remaining to taunt the intellect like a swarm of African bees," said one. Or, "Anger elevated to poetry," said another who was not paid by the word.

Only twice had Bob ever tried to disturb the status quo between himself and his muse.

The first time, when Sean Penn and Oliver Stone bought the movie rights to a particularly disturbing column for a great deal of money, Bob tried to give some of the profits to Buster, but the poor bum (excuse me, "street person") just left it sitting on the sidewalk (after deducting just enough to buy a box of wine at the Pump'n Munch.) Luckily, the bag of cash was found and returned to Bob by the incredibly honest Hieronymus Snoqualmie, chief embalmer at the Sunset Memorial Cemetery and Snoqualmie Funeral Home. So, instead of trying to pay Buster for his contribution to the wonderfully successful enterprise, Bob just fed him a good meal each night and paid Ronaldo Poletski down at the appliance store to put a fresh cardboard box in Buster's alley once a month, a little more often when it rained.

The second time was when the first collection of "The Screed," "F*** This Book," climbed onto the New York Times Bestseller List. Bob had taken the first royalty check (for more money than

Huck Puhzz made in two years) and dragged Buster over to the Holiday Inn Express, where he'd showered him and tried to get him to put on clean clothes and use the bed. As they'd proceeded Buster had stopped ranting and became unusually quiet. When Bob yanked on Buster's overcoat, wondering if it was possible that the lapels had grown together permanently, Buster had suddenly spoken his name. "Mr. Thalia." It had taken Bob aback because the words weren't said in Buster's usual reedy voice.

"What!?" he'd asked in surprise.

"You don't really want to do this, do you?" Buster asked, again in a calm clear voice. He'd looked Bob square in the face, which was something Buster never did (because you might be an IRS soul-sucker or, worse, a Mason.)

The meaning behind the question couldn't have been clearer to Bob Thalia. His career as a rich columnist seemed to melt before his eyes, the autograph parties and author tours vanishing like phantoms. The special retouched dust-jacket photographs faded into oblivion and the free subscription to Interview went flying off to someone else's mailbox. He didn't have to think for very long before he answered.

"No," he'd said to Buster, "no, I guess I don't." Then Bob paid for the room and they left the hotel and went back down to the Eureka! for a bowl of soup and maybe some pie.

That, then, is how Bob Thalia and Buster K.

Whatever became permanent fixtures at the coffee shop in McKinleyville and why, if you stop by J.J.'s Bookstore, you'll find at least fifteen different dailies publishing their highly eccentric column (as well as an entire stack of autographed copies of the book.)

None of this has, so far at least, anything to do with Huck Puhzz and his campaign for mayor, but it's nice to fill out the background a bit and, besides, as I'm sure you have probably already guessed, Bob & Buster will shortly reenter our tale.

V
The Very First Mister Fletcher
In which the tale of the black widow first is spun

With Larry, his campaign manager, taking care of all the legal paperwork, Huck was free to concentrate on creating a political identity for himself in the upcoming election for mayor. He decided he'd try enlisting the help of a real, bona fide writer to help write his speeches. And since there was only one bona fide writer in the county, Huck drove on down to the Eureka!-I-Found-It Coffee Shop to await the arrival of Mr. Bob Thalia and his muse Buster.

Bob showed up a half hour before Buster, as he usually did, so Huck hit him up right away. Concerning Huck's candidacy for mayor, Bob felt at best doubtful. He said he'd need to know a few things about Huck's politics before he could consider helping Huck craft a speech or two. (Truth was, speechwriting was the one area of prose Bob Thalia hadn't yet conquered, and he thought it might be fun to use Huck as a scratch pad.)

"What do you stand for?" he asked Huck. Huck said he didn't know but that he would think about it. "What do you intend to do as mayor?" Bob queried. Huck said he wasn't quite sure, but that whatever he did it would be better than what those real-estate agents and lawyers had been doing (this last bit he'd gotten from Larry.)

"Huck, why exactly is it that you want to run for mayor? Don't you have any political agenda?" Bob finally demanded, frustrated. I mean, if he was going to do this he wanted a scratch pad, not a black hole.

"I'm doing it for the big bucks," Huck told him. There was a long silence and then Bob Thalia slowly spun his stool around so that it faced the pie cabinet. After that, no matter what Huck said, Bob Thalia refused to talk to him anymore. Buster finally came in and started a rant and Bob had to start writing it down. Once Buster showed up Bob was as good as deaf to anybody else.

Huck was devastated, and he moved down the counter to where Alverna Kettle was eating some chicken and peas. He was drowning his sorrow in a cold beer when she leaned over to him and whispered conspiratorially, "Why you running for mayor right now of all times, Puhzz?"

Huck considered this for a moment and then asked Alverna to promise that, if he told her, she wouldn't whisper a word of it to anybody. She nodded, but it was a useless thing to ask of Alverna Kettle. She was McKinleyville's biggest gossip, capable of getting a rumor spread from one end of town to the other, without missing a soul, in under two hours. If there was a piece of dirt you wanted spread around all you had to do was tell Alverna Kettle.

"Mayor Fletcher's son Victor is a thief, narcotics dealer, and general reprobate, and I have the goods on him so she won't say boo about me during the campaign. I expect that I'll win pretty easy, since at the same time I'll be busy painting her as a charlatan and a used car salesman."

Alverna's eyes grew big and she looked both ways as if they were being watched, but for the moment the rest of the clientele was ignoring them. She leaned in close so that her face was inches from Huck's. "Good God, boy, you haven't already told the widow this plan of yours, now, have you?" Huck paused.

"Well, yeah, I left a message at City Hall for her. But it was anon-y-mous." Alverna threw up her hands and then covered her head.

"Jesus, boy, you have put yourself in dutch now! Don't you know she's the widow? You're gonna be A-number-one on her list. You're good as a dead man right this instant." Huck shook his head in confusion. Alverna looked both ways again, ducking as a few colorful obscenities flew by from Buster, and then she led Huck to a dark corner booth in the back.

"Victoria Maria Stanton Christopher Sanders Fletcher is a stone-cold-blooded killer," she told him when they were alone. "The first one she did in was poor old Ben Christopher, who'll never replace a radio tube again. And you may be her next!" To his everlasting regret, Huck asked Alverna what exactly she was talking about and Alverna, of course, told him. That was how he learned the story of the first Mister Fletcher.

Ben Christopher, back in the 60s and 70s, owned The Record Needle, the county's biggest TV and stereo store. Business at The Record Needle had always been pretty good, much of it due to Ben's charming and thorough customer service, so he made a good living. He was well-loved in the community, too. Every season he sponsored a little league team, and every year he was the team leader for the American Cancer Society's "Bowl-Against-Breast Cancer" fundraising drive. As a member of the community he was more than upstanding, and as a bachelor he was a prime choice for the single ladies who were out looking.

When, in the summer of '74, he traded two TVs, a stereo, and two dumptruck loads of landfill brick to Pedro Watanabe for a baby blue 1963 Lincoln Continental, well, women's heads really started to turn. He would cruise up and down Central Avenue in front of The Needle on "Cruise For Jerry's Kids" nights in that baby blue Lincoln, playing Tom Jones and Barry Manilow real loud on his shiny new 8-track player. If he was in the mood he'd call out the names of the ladies he knew firsthand. As Betty Jean Essex said on many an occasion (hanky in hand), Ben Christopher "cut quite a figure."

About this time, "Vickie" Marie Stanton returned from her college graduation in San Francisco. A physically beautiful woman, although with a bit of a shrewish voice, Victoria was not like most of us... picking and feeling our way through life, always learning valuable life lessons a bit too late, making ends meet and going on instinct. No, she already had a complete future in mind for herself. It involved wealth, influence, social status, and a really really nice car. So when she saw Ben Christopher cruising up Central Avenue in that Lincoln and playing Tom Jones she knew she'd found a Humboldt County mover and shaker, and she set out quick to make him her husband.

It took three weeks.

In six months time the two of them had a big house out in Cutten (where the real estate agents and lawyers lived), Victoria was pregnant with Victor, and they were having regular Saturday night parties so big they had to be catered. It was everything Victoria had always wanted, although it wasn't quite the life that Ben had been planning. Still, during the next couple of years his wife was happy, he had a son, and the ocean at Clam Beach looked particularly beautiful to him when he drove out there to relax every Sunday morning. Things could be worse. So he settled on suffering a little so that he could achieve the American Dream.

Then came the late '70s and the Centerton Mall.

When the Mall opened it wiped out seventy-five per cent of McKinleyville's locally owned retail shops. (Huck's campaign manager Larry would have said "I told you so!" if he knew that, back when the zoning permits for the Mall went up before the Board of Supervisors - even though every sane person in the county said it would be ruinous for the local economy - the real estate agents and lawyers on the board voted the Mall through. Of course, they did so mostly because it would be very good for the economy of real estate agents and lawyers.)

Ben bravely tried to match the "At-Cost" sales that The Cheap Guys and Circuit Barn had, but when the rent came due and it was time to pay John, his lone employee (and career electronics expert), the cash flow always got tight. Shortly after the advent of the CD, unfortunately, things at The Record Needle started to slow down even more, possibly because of the bad luck of his business's name.

Then, as if things weren't bad enough, the Wal-Mart in Centerton opened (thanks to the real estate agents and lawyers on the Centerton City Council.)

Victoria wasn't happy at all when the Karoke machine and the new Volvo were repossessed. She was very upset when Ben told her that they'd have to take Victor out of the private school and put him into a regular Kindergarten class. And she was livid when he stopped paying for her Modern Make-Up Selection Of The Month subscription. She slapped him across the face when he told her that they couldn't afford to maintain the pool and rock garden any longer (since both were very popular at social events.) She would have been really furious if she'd known he had sold his golf clubs and used the money to sponsor one last little league team.

It was clear to Victoria that Ben Christopher wasn't the "mover & shaker" she originally thought he was, and she reminded him of his inadequacy at every opportunity, complaining and berating him in a voice that could scare away the fingernails and chalkboards. "You're a vacuum tube!" she would yell at him. "You're obsolete! Why, oh why didn't I marry someone who was going somewhere?" In front of their friends she complained, "He's a eunuch! An idiot! I can't imagine what I ever saw in him!"

At the same time Ben realized she was right in saying that his career was over, and he started to suspect that his marriage had been a mistake as well. Both the store and his wife seemed like weights hanging from his arms or bars caging him in this prison he had made for himself. Victoria was heard saying more than once, at their increasingly cheaper Saturday evening parties, that she wished Ben would drop dead.

So he did.

Well, actually he went down to The Record Needle one Saturday night (just after one of Victoria's parties - she said later that she'd gone to bed.) Then he very deliberately took a stripped wire leading from an amplifier's power unit in each hand and turned on the juice. His suicide note, recorded on one of the store's cassette decks (which had been marked down), expressed his love for Victor and gave his respects to his brother in Ukiah. Then he said goodbye to the world in general. Sheriff Wadd later played back Ben's last words in Dolby Stereo. "I'm dead inventory, nothing but damaged goods. Only one way to get rid of that. Well, folks, I'm 60% off... 70% off... 80% off... 90% off... *free* at last..."

Victoria made enough on the insurance settlement that she put Victor back into private school, got the pool boy back, and bought a considerable amount of stock in the Modern Make-Up Selection Of The Month company. And it was during the community's outpouring of sympathy and goodwill for her family's loss, Alverna told Huck, that Victoria set her claws into the next Mr. Fletcher.

VI
The Fall From The Top Of The World
In which a man tries to touch the sky

Well, Huck told Alverna Kettle he thought the story of the first Mister Fletcher, which she had just finished telling him, was a sad tale and all that, but he didn't quite see what it had to do with his running for mayor. Alverna paused while a loud clatter of dishes from the coffee shop's kitchen disrupted the babble of conversation filling the room and then she leaned in close.

"But that was just the first, Huck. That was just the first." And to Huck's increasing dismay, she told him the even more extraordinary story of the second Mister Fletcher.

After the death of her first husband, "Vickie" Fletcher rebounded quickly, and this time she wasn't going to misinterpret the social position of the man in question. She went straight to the top, and by Christmas had married McKinleyville's mayor.

Harland Sanders was more than just the town's mayor, he was old blood. The Sanders had arrived in Humboldt County even before the Snoqualmies. The family myth that was passed down to the grandchildren and through the press releases that Harland's Automobile Dealership passed out, told how old one-legged great-granddaddy Colonel Matthew Sanders rode into the county in 1883 in a covered wagon and started a blacksmith shop. That much was true, except they left out that he was running from the law because he was a horse thief. The Colonel had lost his leg in the civil war, the story continued, and he'd cast himself a new leg out of iron, with a hinge at the knee. Of course, an iron leg would probably weigh so much that two healthy men couldn't get it off the ground, but that was the story and the Sanders family stuck with it. When the automobile revolution came along Matt and his sons made the transition from blacksmithing to auto assembly and repair and eventually started selling cars, which is where that old family horse-thieving knowhow came in handy. To this day you can't miss Sanders Auto City if you drive up US 52, because of the huge neon letters "SANDERS AUTO CITY" resting on a two-story tall iron leg.

By the time Harland was born he was Humboldt County royalty and didn't really have to work for his supper. Besides, he didn't care much for cars. He thought the investments his brothers were involved with were boring too. He was an anxious sort of guy, always on the move, always eager to move on to the next 'really big thing.' So, after numerous forays into a variety of professions, he decided to try politics (which again took advantage of the traditional family talent.) His family said it was a "Harland thing" but supported him with their considerable wealth and influence.

The year that Ben Christopher marked himself down to zero, Harland Sanders held his big campaign for mayor. A huge circus tent was erected at the Auto City and a seven day rally was held ("Come meet your next mayor under the Big Top at the Big Iron Leg," the ads suggested.) Harland's speeches were unremarkable, but the free beer and the music of the Jazz Monsters (who drove over from Centerton) kept people coming back. By Election Day no one could even remember his opponent's name. And Victoria Maria Stanton Christopher had found her new man.

At first their lives went along swimmingly. Harland cared for Victor and raised him like his own son. He did a fair job as mayor, although he quickly found that it bored him as well. And Victoria moved into the only house in the county that might be considered a "mansion," where she held her Saturday night parties catered by Le Food, Centerton's gourmet restaurant (very small portions, but laid out on the plate so artistically you hated to move the pea.) There were really really nice cars in the garage, and every Tuesday a maid cleaned the house.

In fact, Victoria's life of snobbish perfection would probably have continued forever if it hadn't been for one Galadriel Windstar.

Galadriel had originally come to Humboldt County to finish college, live at the Last Rainbow Commune, and have easy access to the evil weed - in reverse order. She dressed simply, in airy cotton skirts that fell to her feet, natural off-white cotton blouses given color by tie-dyed scarves draped in appropriate places, Birkenstock sandals on her feet, and a khaki backpack forever hanging from her shoulders. She carried with her at all times the indelicate scent of patchouli oil, her wavy blond hair usually had at least one flower or piece of colored yarn weaved into it, and she moved with the slow grace of the perpetually stoned. But once she arrived beneath the towering redwood trees she had a conversion to a new religion.

Galadriel went to work for the Defenders Of Our Mother Earth (DOOME), a sister organization to the Mothers Against Greedy International Corporations (MAGIC) which had, despite a less friendly title, a much friendlier acronym. She started handing out environmental pamphlets between her classes and she frequently stopped pedestrians with questions like, "Did you know only God can make a tree?" or "What if the solar system is just part of an atom in some giant's fingernail?" Well, she didn't always stick to the subject. Then one day she saw Mayor Harland Sanders crossing Central Avenue and stopped him.

It's hard to say whether it was the girl or the pamphlet that captured Harland's fancy. Or maybe it was Harland's anxious desire to move on to the "next really big thing." But within a few days he had undergone a transformation much more remarkable than the girl's. He started protesting old growth clear-cuts during city council meetings, held tirades against local timber companies during ribbon-cuttings and worst, as far as Victoria was concerned, he gave away their hard-earned money to environmental groups. She didn't care if some musty four-thousand-year-old soon-to-be-stump got protected for a few more months or not, but she did care that the family could continue to afford having the massage therapist come by three times a week.

Harland's conversion even started to bother the rest of the family. He would sit in the Auto City office beneath the big neon clock ("...Big Iron Leg time is four-twenty-two...") and tell his brothers how they had to keep oil and other toxic and petroleum products spilled at the repair shop from washing into the ground water. He had them dig up an ancient, buried and almost-forgotten junk pile because there might be lead and asbestos in it. And, most horrifying to the Auto City's employees, he made them use recycled toilet paper.

Finally Victoria came face-to-face with Harland and demanded that he stop siphoning off so much of their funds for "the Greens" as she called them. "I'm not losing the jacuzzi so that some ugly bird can build a nest!" This upset Harland, since he'd been thinking that she would eventually see the light just as he had. But he still harbored hope. That very morning Galadriel had stopped by City Hall with a proposal that might help him convert poor deluded Victoria. So Harland made Victoria a deal.

"The Group," (which was what Harland called them), "is going on a backpacking trip to get back in touch with Our Mother Earth's roots," he said. "We're going to climb Horse Mountain and hold a ritual in which each of us touches the sky. Victoria, come with us! If you still feel the way you do now when we return I'll cut my donations to The Group in half!"

So that was how Harland Sanders, mayor of McKinleyville, got his wife Victoria, who had never been anywhere wilder than the County Fair, to backpack into the deeps of the Trinity Mountains with a motley crew of environmentalists, naturalists, and ex-hippies.

The following sunny Saturday found this passel of people at "base camp," two miles below the craggy peak of Horse Mountain. It's hard to say whether it was the beautiful blue sky or his desire to see Victoria transformed, or possibly once again his anxiousness about moving on to the "next really big thing," but Harland dragged Victoria out of their tent early to get a head start up the mountain. Victoria would surely have protested louder if she hadn't still been half-asleep, and before she was completely awake they were half way up the trail.

One positive thing (and only one) may be said about Victoria Maria Stanton Christopher Sanders at this juncture. All those privately coached workouts at the gym and hours spent using the stairmaster and buttmaster (although these were motivated by vanity) kept her fit and capable of keeping up with

The Return Of The Teapot Dome

Harland during the arduous climb. As a matter a fact, she was healthy enough that she had breath to spare, yelling at and cursing Harland the whole way.

"You pitiful moron! They're just stealing your money! It's all done by outside agitators!" she said. "If they stop cutting down the trees none of us will have toilet paper, except for that recycled crap you've forced them to use down at Auto City!" she told him. "If the mill closes the town will go bankrupt, you'll lose your job, and they'll repossess everything we have!" she warned. "If you give them one more penny I'll divorce you and air every bit of dirty laundry you have in the press! I'll bring you down and your damn family!" she threatened. It became clear that the trip had wrought no changes to Victoria's state of mind.

Harland remained silent throughout all of this, smelling the delicate fragrances in the warm forest breeze, listening to the hoots and chirps of the birds concealed in the foliage above them, and absorbing the spirit of Our Mother Earth. The moisture in the grass beneath his feet seeped upward through his body and he felt more alive than he had in four blue moons and a coon's age. Already he felt separated from his former life among auto repairmen, investors, and politicians back in the city. This cathedral of nature, he knew, was where he belonged.

As they rose above timberline into the unforgiving altitudes of rock and wind atop the mountain's peak, Harland began to really hoof it and left Victoria far behind, or at least that was what happened according to the statement she made to Sheriff Wadd later that day. She watched him ascend the sharp slab that capped the mountain and jutted out over the sheer face and twelve hundred foot drop on the opposite side. She said she saw Harland straining onto his tiptoes at the highest point and stretch his arms up into the air. And then he was gone.

The Group, which was several hundred yards further down the trail, said they also saw Harland on the peak, arms high above his head, but some said they saw a second figure next to him and others said they did not.

Either way, every member of The Group agreed with Victoria concerning what they had heard. Just before Harland vanished over the precipice he had bellowed out in his loudest voice, "I can touch the sky!"

His father later said to Ken Feedleman, in a sad but contented sort of voice, "Well, Harland probably just wanted to move on to the next really big thing."

Victoria got more than just an insurance settlement this time. She became an equal owner in Sanders Auto City. She received several hundred thousand dollars in investments that Harland had made before he got bored with banking and investment. And, when the runoff election was held in McKinleyville to seat a mayor for the rest of

Harland's term, Victoria won by a landslide.

She of course terminated the Harland Sanders Environmental Education Fund with extreme prejudice.

VII
Why Frying Pans Are Not Good For Disciplining Children
In which the power of parenthood is once again abused

The jist of the tales Alverna Kettle was telling in the dark corner of the Eureka!-I-Found-It Coffee Shop started becoming clear to Huck Puhzz. There was the distinct possibility, Alverna was suggesting, that Victoria Maria Stanton Christopher Sanders Fletcher, mayor of McKinleyville, had brutally murdered her last two husbands because they got in the way of her ambition. And the person who had just that morning sent a letter threatening Mayor Victoria Fletcher's ambition was Huck. A cold dread settled between Huck's ears.

"But what about the other candidates for mayor?" he asked Alverna. She guffawed and slurped up some of Art's six-hour-old burnt-bean java.

"There isn't anybody else running, excepting Seamus Malloy and now you," she pointed out. "Nobody else will run against her."

"Maybe she'll think Seamus sent the letter," Huck said hopefully. Alverna guffawed again.

"Seamus? Seamus Malloy? He couldn't string enough letters together to spell 'dick,'" she said. "Don't you know about Seamus Malloy?" Huck admitted that he didn't. So...

Okay, folks, let me stop here for a minute, because I know what you're thinking. You're getting antsy. This makes four flashback stories in a row and you want to get on with the main event and find out what the consequences of Huck running for mayor were. Well, keep your pants on for one more story, and then we'll get on with things. Huck kept his patience. He sat there absolutely spellbound while Alverna Kettle told him the entire strange saga of young Seamus Malloy.

Everybody knew the Malloy Boys, whose names (in alphabetical order, since at the time I tell this tale all seem as if they are about thirty-two) were Blaine, Cedric, Cassidy, Colm, Cowan, Desmond, Devlin, Ennis, Gallagher, Killian, Riddock, Riordan, Rowan, Seamus, Sean, and Walter. Their Momma had an Irish brogue so thick molasses seemed thin, but the boys had lived around it for so long none of them noticed it any more. In fact they frequently got into fistfights with other boys in the neighborhood just because the offenders had suggested the boys' mamma had an accent. Some of the brothers were no doubt adopted, although they were all topped with brilliant red hair and could easily have been related. The family clung to its Irish heritage proudly, opening a shop that sold nothing but goods imported from Ireland in Centerton's touristy dock district, sponsoring a Celtic Rock band that played Sundays at the Jambalaya night club, and, of course, seven of the boys went into police work as a vocation. The Anti-Irish Defamation League had once written the family a letter complaining that they were reinforcing too many stereotypes.

Unfortunately, Poppa Malloy died young, kicked in the unmentionables by a sheep, and that left Momma Malloy alone to raise their sixteen rambunctious boys. And when the boys started getting out of control Momma frequently resorted to her favorite form of punishment; the frying pan.

When the boys did something disagreeable Momma would whack them on the rear, leg, hand, elbow, head, or whatever body part was available with a cast iron frying pan. Nowadays we might think of such treatment as abuse and give the social workers a call, but back in the days when Momma Malloy was brought up, spanking and switching and getting whipped with a belt were socially acceptable forms of parental discipline. In her defense, I might also note that the Malloy boys became exceptionally well behaved (except when jerks suggested their mother had an accent.) Frying Pan Therapy was rarely required. And not one of the boys was any the worse for the wear, at least at first.

Then one day, back when Seamus was about five (give or take), that changed. He trotted happily out the door to go to school right after Momma had beaned him on the noggin with the big iron spider for refusing to eat his oatmeal before it got cold. As he skipped down the street with four of his brothers he turned back and called out, "Love you, Momma!"

And those were the last words Seamus Malloy would say to his mother for better than thirty years.

When Seamus got home that afternoon he was as mum as a statue. He'd open his mouth to shovel food into it and to get a good deep breath, but otherwise his lips were sealed. No amount of questioning, cajoling, teasing by his siblings, or threats with the frying pan could get him to open his mouth and utter a sound. He remained mute until bedtime, and the next day was the same and so was the next day after that.

Abraham Siusse, the family's doctor, couldn't explain it. He took x-rays, blood samples, urine samples, stool samples, MRIs and EEGs. He brought in specialists from San Francisco and Sacramento and sent the test results to labs way back on the East Coast. But they all said the same thing. There wasn't anything physically wrong with Seamus. He just wasn't talking.

The family tried taking Seamus to old Bob Hartley, the children's psychologist who worked part time and painted pictures of redwoods down in Garberville. After ten sessions he gave up on Seamus, mostly because he wanted to finish a new watercolor of the Eel River and a particularly beautiful redwood grove. But he admitted he didn't think that there was anything wrong with the boy. The kid just didn't want to talk and there wasn't anything wrong with that, as far as he was concerned. He did, however, suggest that Seamus try different forms of communication. Perhaps something like painting.

Momma, of course, blamed herself. She was positive that she'd done some kind of permanent brain damage to poor little Seamus with that last whack with the frying pan. She retired the thing (much to the boys' delight) and replaced it with stern hour-long lectures (much to the boys' dismay.) And every night she'd retire to her boudoir, sit on the edge of her bed with a framed picture of Seamus - frozen at five years of age forever thanks to Kodak - and then she would cry herself to sleep.

Well, over the years little Seamus Malloy grew up into big Seamus Malloy. He did fairly well in school, at least for a boy who wouldn't talk. Other than a few taunts like "Hey, Marcel Marceau!" and "I know you're not deaf, but are you dumb?" from Hunsey Bourcarte, he got through High School relatively unscathed. And when, after he graduated with a modest 2.5 grade point average, he was hired at the Big Loaf Bakery to deliver bread to local grocery stores he did a very good (if very quiet) job.

One evening, more than thirty years after he'd

spoken those last words to his Momma, Seamus came knocking on the door of his brother Cassidy's house. Cass's wife Jeanne worked as a day care provider for the children of all the other Malloy Brothers (twenty-seven tykes at last count.) Each day around five-thirty the brothers who had kids (meaning everybody but Seamus) stopped by after work to pick them up and hang around for a beer. When Jeanne let Seamus in that day and he joined the others around the kitchen table the entire sixteen-brother clan had come together. When Seamus came in they were talking about the relative merits of the movie *"Titanic"*, McKinleyville's notorious city garbage contract, and the so-far unopposed reelection of Victoria Maria Stanton Christopher Sanders Fletcher to the seat of mayor. Everyone in the room froze when Seamus loudly cleared his throat.

"I want to run against Vickie Stanton for mayor," he said.

You could have knocked everyone in the room over with a feather. They hadn't heard Seamus speak in three decades. Still more shocking, they'd never heard him speak in the booming bass grown-up voice that he used now. To make sure they'd actually heard him he repeated what he'd said. But they'd heard him alright.

"Will you help?" he added.

There was a helluva lot of whooping, cheering and hollering in Cassidy and Jeanne's kitchen that day, my friends, and I'll just leave it at that. And when Momma found out, well, you could hear her in Bridgeville.

The Malloy Family network went into high gear to elect Seamus as McKinleyville's next mayor. They posted banners and signs on every corner. They had rallies at every pub from the Mendocino County line in the south to the Del Norte County line to the north. But the effort seemed a futile one. Seamus, although he spoke now occasionally to his brothers when absolutely necessary, still refused to utter a word in public and, as far as Cedric (his campaign publicity manager) could ascertain, he had no political opinions at all (except that Big Loaf Bakery drivers should be able to start work at 5:00am, because 4:00am was too early.) None of the brothers was even sure why he was running for mayor at all. But they were determined to get him elected if it kept him talking.

In fact, the only person Seamus talked to regularly was Momma. Finally, after decades of guilt and anguish over what she might have done to poor Seamus with that old iron frying pan, he told her the truth about his silence. He told her the truth about his muteness and also why he had decided to speak once more and why he wanted to run for mayor. And these things not even Alverna Kettle knew.

On that pivotal day, thirty years before, little five-year-old Seamus had gone skipping off to school, and when he got there he had been subjected to the cruelest words ever spoken to him in his whole short life. Words so cruel that he chose not to ever speak again himself so that he could never by chance utter words so biting, hurtful, and hateful.

Words spoken by vindictive, mean-spirited little nine-year-old Victoria Maria Stanton.

VIII
Huck Looks For Protection
In which the Federal Government is, as usual, of no help

When Huck Puhzz got back to the Pump'n Munch to check in with his brother Bubba and Mayoral Campaign Manager, Larry, he was shakin' like a leaf. The tales of death surrounding his opponent, 'Black Widow' Victoria Fletcher, which Alverna Kettle had shared with him, had disturbed him more than if he'd heard Vanna White had quit *Wheel Of Fortune*.

When he arrived at the gas station/convenience store most of the posse was behind the service counter. Big Kenny was rotating the whole chickens in the Display Roaster, looking for the one with the biggest breasts. Hampton and Sammy had that morning's donuts and crullers (now considered day-old since it was after midnight) spread out on a

The Return Of The Teapot Dome

piece of butcher paper on the floor and they were currently picking the sprinkles off of several rainbow-colored ones. Little Larry was working the cash register, even though he wasn't officially an employee of the store. And Larry and Bubba were seated at one of the snackin' tables drinking beers and playing gin rummy. As Huck came in they both entered into a drunken off-key rendition of "Hail To The Chief" that petered out after the first few notes because they forgot how the song went.

In short order Huck told Bubba and Larry everything that Alverna had told him down at the coffee shop. Well, actually just the parts that he remembered, but that was enough.

"What're you gonna do, Huck?" Sammy asked from the floor by the register. "She's gonna kill you for sure, with you having the goods on Victor and all. Why don't you just give up?"

"Gruesome ways to die," Big Kenny pointed out. "One falls off a mountain and goes splat, kind of jellyfied. Other one's electrocuted, all fried like a chicken." He removed a plump bird from the roaster, leaving a trail of grease on the counter. "Bubba, can I pay for this tomorrow?"

"There are worse ways to die," Hampton said. "I know a guy who knew a guy whose uncle was tryin' to get away from his wife for a few hours, you know, to get some peace of mind. So one night he drove his Volkswagen bug out to the end of the south jetty, just when a storm was brewing. He just sat there in the car, you know, eatin' Twix bars and drinking cranberry juice and readin' Hemmings Motor News. The waves along the bar just kept gettin' higher and higher as the storm come sneakin' in, but he didn't notice. Then a big one hits and BOOM! The whole car was gone, guy and all, swept out to sea."

Larry snorted. "You think getting washed out to sea is worse than falling off a mountain or getting fried?"

"Sure. Getting fried is, like, over in a second. But the car has air in it, see, so when it goes down you get to breathe for a while before you drown, screaming and flailing. You see it coming." Hampton held up a hand filled with about two-hundred colored candy flakes. "Anybody want a sprinkle?"

"Right," Larry argued as he walked over for a pinch of sprinkles, "you don't think a guy falling off a mountain doesn't have time to see it coming? All the way down to the ground, five hundred feet, he's screamin', those big old rocks are rushing up to meet him. SMACK! That's painful. Volkswagen bug gets carried out to sea, it's night so it's gonna be dark, the windows'll blow out, you get sucked out of the car and you're drowned. Seems like sort of a peaceful death, really."

Huck held up his hands. "Look, guys, I don't want peaceful death or any other kind of death. What am I gonna do?"

Bubba, who had remained silent throughout

the conversation, finally spoke up. "Don't the government protect people that's running for electoral office? All them Secret Service guys with the little phones in their ears and the uzis hidden in their jackets?"

"Say, that's right, them guys that was all standing around Reagan when he got shot," Sammy agreed.

"And those guys running alongside Kennedy's car when he was killed," Larry said. "Yeah, you could use some of those."

Huck brightened up for the first time since he had arrived. He climbed over Hampton and Sammy and ducked between Little Larry's legs to get the phone directory from beneath the register so that he could look up the Secret Service.

He couldn't find a listing at first, but finally one of the boys, who had paid a tiny bit more attention than the rest of the posse in civics class (before dropping out of high school) remembered that the Secret Service was a part of the Department of the Treasury. So Huck looked for that. He found the number in the Government Pages under "Secret Service US, San Francisco Field Office." He scratched it with a knife in the gray rub-off stuff on a losing lottery ticket and stuck it in his front pocket. He was feeling better already.

The next morning Huck got out of bed, rubbed his teeth with his fingers, fed Whizzer some leftover spaghetti, and then dialed 1-415-744-9026.

(Warning: Please do not attempt this at home. This is the actual telephone number of the US Secret Service from the actual phone book, and if you dial it without a reason you may annoy the Secret Service. And you really don't want the Secret Service annoyed at you.)

The nice woman who answered the phone listened as Huck explained his candidacy for mayor, the bad luck Mayor Fletcher's husbands had experienced, and described the kind of danger he believed he was in. Just between you and me, the nice woman didn't laugh, per se, but had seemed to have "trouble breathing" during several key parts of Huck's story. When he was finished she thanked him for calling...

"...but we only deal with candidates for federal office, Mr. Puhzz. I'm afraid municipal elections fall outside our jurisdiction. I would recommend calling your city police or, if you feel they are compromised, your county sheriff." Huck considered his record with Sheriff Kearney, including the notorious night at the Chinese Baptist Church, and dismissed the idea.

"What if they're all in league with her?" he asked. The nice woman had another bout of difficulty breathing.

"You... ah... could try the District Attorney if you think a law has actually been broken. Or perhaps you could drop out of the election if you feel you are in that much jeopardy. Thank you for calling, Mr. Puhzz." She coughed slightly. "Good luck."

The Return Of The Teapot Dome

And then the line went dead. Dead like Huck figured he was going to be pretty soon.

Huck didn't need to dress, seeing as how he'd slept in his clothes (for security reasons), so he gathered up his odds and ends and headed out to the pickup. At least he wasn't going to stay at home alone waiting to be picked off like a sitting duck. He'd drive on in to the Pump'n Munch and hang out with Rupert, the day manager. As long as he stayed in crowds it would be harder for the Mayor to knock him off, he figured.

He was almost to the truck when he saw the old Chrysler parked on the road just south of his driveway. Nobody else lived around here, so there was no cause for a car to be there. And the last time Huck had spied a car sitting there... well, within minutes he had been surrounded by half the town's population, a cartload of vigilantes, and the sheriff, all with their sights locked on him.

He crouched as low as his ailing back would let him and scurried up to the pickup. Luckily the driver's door faced his trailer and not the road, so he opened the door unseen and squeezed into the cab as quietly as he could. This was no casual skulker, he knew. But the Mayor wouldn't do her own dirty work, that's for sure.

"Hit men!" he thought suddenly, and the icy grip of cold-fingered fear or whatever grabbed him. Why, oh why hadn't he read more of those Robert Ludlum books? He'd have been better prepared for this sort of thing. Quietly he stepped on the clutch, released the brake and, keeping his head low to avoid any flying bullets, rolled down his driveway toward US 52 in neutral. Four potholes later he started the engine and popped it into gear, squealing onto the highway and almost colliding with a mail truck.

Just before it fell out of view in his rear-view mirror Huck saw the dark-colored-Chrysler pull out, make a u-turn, and start after him.

IX
The Return Of The Teapot Dome
In which the angel of death comes for Huck Puhzz

Huck pulled his truck up in front of the Pump'n Munch and he left it sitting crookedly across two parking spaces. He knew that the dark-colored-Chrysler, filled with hit men employed by his arch-nemesis Mayor Victoria Fletcher, would be arriving momentarily. He cursed the moment he had been inspired to run for mayor. He should have known this would be the outcome! Politics was the domain of ruthless people, killers, lawyers, and real estate agents. Small potatoes like him, an average Joe millworker on disability, were between-meal-snacks for these Machiavellian monsters.

Rupert the Pump'n Munch day manager, a graduate of American Correspondence Schools' mail-order course in retail management, was busy scrubbing down the counter with Clorox and making new donuts, crullers, and roasted chickens when the door flew open. He was surprised when Huck came bursting in, since Huck almost never came by until after Bubba's shift had started.

"If any guys come in here looking for me I ain't here," Huck told Rupert, and he grabbed two magazines from the front rack and then disappeared into the stock room.

"Even if it's Bubba?" Rupert asked too late, just as the door clicked shut. Across the street the notorious dark-colored-Chrysler parallel-parked (very neatly), but no one got out.

"It's hit men! Hired by Mayor Fletcher, come to kill me because I threatened to expose her son!" Huck told Bubba when his brother arrived for the beginning of the evening management shift. He indicated the car of evil, which still sat menacingly across the street from the Pump'n Munch. Bubba thought for a moment and then went outside and walked across the street. He stood by the vehicle of doom for a minute and then returned.

"Nobody in it now," he told Huck.

"But there was! I tell you, they're following me and they're going to kill me, just like Ben Christopher and Harland Sanders!" Huck cried, jumping up and down and occasionally ducking behind the Little Debbie Cakes & Pies rack.

"Then stay in back and I'll keep an eye out," Bubba said, pulling two six-packs out of the store's cooler for the evening's posse-party and hauling them to the freezer in the back alley. Huck reluctantly shuffled off to the stock room and sat on the floor next to the brooms, where he already had a stack of reading material. It wasn't the perfect hideout since the stock room had no door on it, but it was better than sitting out in the open waiting for a sharpshooter to take him out.

Sitting on the stock room floor of a convenience store next to the mops, brooms, and foul-smelling buckets sure wasn't quite what Huck had expected when he'd first launched his glamorous campaign for mayor. But nobody ever said politics was pretty.

The moment of truth came quicker than Huck had figured. About fifteen minutes later the posse arrived together (the monster truck rally had just let out) and Bubba told them about the dark-colored Chrysler that had been following Huck all day and was still parked across the Highway from the Pump'n Munch. Bubba said it was only a matter of time before these expert hit men tracked Huck down in the stock room.

"It's gonna be a might quicker than that," Little Larry said, "unless he gets back in there behind the brooms and we put the big Coca-Cola bikini lady display in front of him. All the candidates are out on the stump. Chainsaw Annie's working the patrons of the Junk Garden Antique Boutique and Mayor Fletcher and her toadies are glad-handing their way up this side of the street right now, passing out propaganda and begging for votes."

"Yup. They'll be here any minute," Larry added.

Well, Huck's face went so white you could have made it into a pretty respectable wedding dress. And if he hadn't used the Pump'n Munch's rather grimy men's facilities just five minutes before he might have had an accident that, due to your active imagination, requires no further description.

"I'm a dead man!" he whispered. But all was not lost, as his resourceful brother jumped into the breach.

"Big Kenny!" Bubba called out. "You get over there next to the front door. No, behind the garbage can. Hampton, grab one of them baseball bats. I don't care if they've got rubber foam on the outside, they'll still knock a gun outta a hit man's hand. No, I get the real wood one. Now get underneath the snackin' tables. Sammy! You duck there behind the popcorn machine. There should be a can of really hot oil. Don't touch it yourself, you idiot! Grab it with a towel so's you can throw it at the hit men! Larry, you and Little Larry sit down inconspicuous-like at the counter. Here are some forks." Bubba became, in this moment of need, an army general. He knew the battleground like the back of his hand, and grabbed the boys and put them in their spots quickly. Within moments they were in place, a crack defensive team, strategically placed where they could best defend Huck, who still cowered in the stock room.

"Where are you gonna hide?" Larry asked from the donut bar stool.

"I don't hide, moron! I work here!" he said, moving behind the cash register and toying with the end of the hardwood baseball bat that he kept for chasing off less-than-experienced robbers.

Then the moment arrived.

The front doors of the Pump'n Munch swung open and a group of four people entered. The three people to the back, two men and a woman, were all clothed in business blue and were loaded down with fliers, pamphlets, and voter registration cards. The woman in the lead, however, was neatly dressed in an expensive pantsuit of black and white, with sparkling earrings and significantly too much makeup. She was still six feet away from Bubba when she extended her arm toward him.

"Mister Pooz," she started, but the man leaned forward and whispered something in her ear and she repeated, "Mister Puhzz."

"Yup?" he said, eyes darting to make sure the Mayor's party hadn't noticed the hidden platoon of defenders.

"I'm your Mayor, Victoria Fletcher, and I'm just checking out the neighborhood making sure that everyone is happy with the city, you know, looking for suggestions from the regular people and keeping in touch." She came close to Bubba, grasping his hand. "It's so important to keep in touch."

"Yup," he said, watching her toadies for suspicious movements.

"You know, my administration was responsible for having all the sidewalks on the waterfront converted to cobblestone," Victoria Fletcher said, batting her eyes.

"Hmph. Seems to me the concrete ones did just fine," Bubba pointed out.

"So, is there anything your Mayor can do for you?" she asked without missing a beat.

"Nope," Bubba answered, taking a gander to make sure Huck was still completely obscured by the great cardboard bikini lady drinking Coke.

"Well, then, can I count on your vote this week?" the Mayor asked, already starting to turn and move toward the door.

"Yup," Bubba said, a clever lie which he hoped felt convincing.

"Thank yew, Mister Pooz," Mayor Fletcher said, and she and her entourage were out the door and halfway to Roxy's Discount Furniture Outlet before Bubba had a chance to blink.

Huck stuck his head out around the die-cut cardboard bottom of the bikini lady and glanced around the Pump'n Munch. "Are they gone?" he asked.

"Gone and done," Bubba replied.

Huck started to dance a bit, the relief being so palpable (big dictionary word) and he ran his fingers through his hair. Maybe he might make it to Election Day alive after all.

"I thought I was a goner for sure!" Huck said. "Did you see how mean that fella she had with her looked? I'll bet you dollars to donuts he was a hit man! He had a bulge —"

"Hold that thought," Bubba interrupted. "Can you pop out the back door to the freezer and grab the two six-packs of Mickey's in the ice tray?" Big Kenny looked beseechingly at Huck from his hiding place next to the front door, and Sammy, unseen behind the popcorn machines called out a muffled "Me too!" Huck sighed and headed for the screen door that opened onto the alley.

And that, as they keep on saying, was unfortunate serendipity.

Huck stopped short of the freezer when he saw something shadowy move in the alley. A dark, ominous figure was hulking behind the store's dumpster. The adrenaline high he'd been on all day ratcheted up four or five notches and he slammed himself back against the wall. The Mayor had moved on, but the hit men were still here! Could he afford to call out for Bubba and the posse? Or would forty-five caliber slugs, fired through those miracle silencers they always have in the movies, *pfft-pfft* him dead before his protectors even heard?

Slowly, carefully, he stuck his head out to peek

into the alley shadows.

And then the attack came.

The ominous figure moved out of the shadows suddenly, quickly, leaving Huck no time to act in his own defense. He turned, just a little, before the wrath of God came down upon him with a deafening crack, and he collapsed to the ground. Pain shot through his limp body and he was barely able to remain conscious.

At first he figured he was dead. That the colors he saw were reflections off the Pearly Gates. But then, dazed, in shock, Huck realized that he was still awake, and that the lump which was growing on his head was throbbing and hurting something fierce. The oscillating purple spots and cascading diamonds continued to dance and spin around him even though he was pretty sure he wasn't moving. An ominous figure still bent over him, and he could feel its hot, fetid breath.

"Alverna Kettle told me you were runnin' for mayor, ya bastard," a voice hissed in a thick Irish brogue. "Well, think again. Nobody is gonna get in the way of me boy and his dreams! You quit, now! Ya hear?"

With that the ominous figure shuffled off down the alley, a huge long-handled cast-iron frying pan hanging from one hand and almost dragging the ground.

"As the sun set, the shadows slowly crawled up the walls of the Pump'n Munch Convenience Store & Gas Mart until any part of the building's exterior not directly illuminated by the cheap flickering fluorescent parking lights had been plunged into an unholy darkness."
    page 155

X
Our Conclusion
In which elections are settled and destiny continues to take its course

After the posse had waited for about a half hour for Huck to show up with the beers they'd sent him out to get they finally got worried. Bubba had them come out of their hiding places and go looking for him. Hampton thought that maybe Huck had run off on them to go steal a sword or a Wheel Of Fortune or an emu again (due to the set of similar circumstances in the tale which has been previously told.) But Bubba doubted it and for a moment thought that maybe Mayor Fletcher's hit men had gotten his poor brother after all.

They found Huck in the first place they looked for him, stunned and bleeding just a bit, lying on the ground next to the Pump'n Munch's spare freezer. While Bubba and Big Kenny hauled Huck in and sat him at one of the snackin' tables Hampton retrieved the beers.

"What happened?" Bubba asked as they put a paper bag full of crushed ice on Huck's head. The lump on Huck's head was big enough to win third place in the 4-H's Annual Biggest Pumpkin, Squash, and Gourd Contest.

"I don't know," Huck said a bit groggily. "Some Irish woman hit me on the head with a frying pan."

"Why?" Larry chimed in.

"I think she said because Alverna Kettle told her to," Huck replied. In his frying-pan addled brain it never occurred to him to put together the story Alverna Kettle had told him just the previous night, about a frying-pan wielding Irish mother, with the facts concerning his Celtic kitchen-implement-wielding attacker. But, considering Huck, does that surprise you?

"A hit man disguised as an Irish woman?" Hampton asked. "That's pretty clever."

"The dark-colored Chrysler is gone," Big Kenny pointed out, and they all went to the front windows to see for themselves. The paper bag on Huck's head, now soaked through, ripped apart and he left a trail of ice chips and water as he moved across the store. Sure enough, the parking spot across from the Pump'n Munch was empty.

"Well I'll be damned," Larry said.

After the initial attack they figured that Huck was safe as long as he just went home and didn't give any running-for-mayor speeches or nothing. Larry threw out the fifty bumper stickers he'd had made up for the campaign (which read "* PUHZZ * BECAUSE *" — Larry liked slogans that rhymed.) Bubba brought Huck's mail out to him every day and Sammy brought him a fifty-gallon-drum of Dennison's Chili, which was finally back in stock at the Bulk Foods Club. Huck and his hound-dog

The Return Of The Teapot Dome

Whizzer just sat in the living room of his trailer each day watching TV and doing the crossword puzzles from the last six-months' Post-Standards, which he'd been meaning to throw out but which had instead turned into a five-foot stack of newsprint beside the water heater.

When Election Day came around and Victoria Fletcher retained her office with a landslide margin Huck finally felt safe again. The next afternoon he got dressed and drove down to the Pump'n Munch to have a beer with the posse and celebrate. He bought a copy of the Post-Standard's post-election edition just out of curiosity to see if he'd gotten any votes.

CITY REAFFIRMS ITS LOVE FOR MAYOR, the headline read. **MAYOR THROWING BIG PARTY THIS SATURDAY NIGHT**, announced another story, which included a complete menu of the catered food for the upcoming bash. The paper described Mayor Fletcher's 96% of the vote and, on the editorial page, the Editor commented that the other four percent of voters, all of whom had voted for Sean Malloy, were most likely in actuality all Malloys and relatives-of-Malloys. If you took into account the considerable size of the family, the Editor wrote, the Malloys took up at least four percent of the population all by themselves. There was no mention in the newspaper at all of any votes for Huck Puhzz.

Of course, there was a good reason for that. You see, Larry had done a very bad job of filling out the paperwork, and he had incorrectly turned it in to City Hall at the Business License desk. The clerk there, upholding the reputation of bureaucrats everywhere, intended to memo it over to the Elections Department as soon as possible, maybe even by sometime in the next month. So, to make a long story short, Huck wasn't even on the ballot. Also unknown to Huck was the fact that Mayor Victoria Fletcher had never seen his note, which had been considered a prank by a secretary and thrown out. In fact she'd never had any idea Huck was running for mayor.

And, of course, none of the posse knew Huck wasn't on the ballot, because none of them bothered to vote.

So Huck went back to his life the way it was before fate had touched him. He missed his big opportunity for greatness, but he'd survived, and at least he had his great "at-the-scene" story of seeing a shoplifter run from J.J.'s Bookstore to tell at parties.

What about Sean Malloy, whose candidacy really lay at the source of Huck's attack? Well, in the Malloy households there was some sadness at the defeat, but Seamus himself took it in stride.

"It's okay, Momma," he said, still willing to talk. "I'll rise above all of this. I just needed to challenge my fears, to make a statement against the tyranny of evil. I lost, but good does lose the battle with sin and malevolence now and again. It just makes the noble that much stronger. I've purged myself of the anger and resentment I held for so long against the individual whose actions drove me into my protracted silence, and now I feel I can move forward with my life. I'm content in the knowledge that I've done my small part to face the pinnacle of wickedness in the eye and decry it, and perhaps now I can pass the mantle of my rebellion on to someone younger in spirit. If each of us was to raise our hands and pledge our words or our silence just once in our lives to fight the cacophony of materialism and hate, then what better world might we live in? A world where every man and woman took personal responsibility for the things they wrought, infusing the world with goodness and brightening the world until there were no more shadows. If we each took just..."

"Shut up," Momma said.

Sean Malloy returned to work driving for the Big Loaf Bakery, and eventually got married and had nine very talkative children of his own.

And that's the story.

Oh, one last thing. On election day, as the sun lowered into the turbulent clouds along the horizon, Kirk Fletcher left his wife's campaign headquarters and took a drive along the marina, watching the sailing and fishing boats as they bobbed in the choppy water. It had been a noisy day, and he'd gone by the house and grabbed one of the vehicles from their eight-car garage for an evening spin. Now that the votes were in and the victory party was in full swing Kirk had decided he didn't really want to be around his wife. She was full of herself, preening and congratulating herself over her landslide win. It was a meaningless victory as far as Kirk was concerned, since there hadn't been a serious challenger. Still, she'd be there with her brown-nosing society acolytes until two or three in the morning and he wanted none of it.

The eucalyptus trees danced in the wind as he drove past them and over the Samoa Bridge, past Woodley Island, Indian Island, and the Coast Guard Station. As he drove up the Samoa Dunes Road the intermittent wail of the North Jetty Lighthouse's foghorn grew louder and louder.

He parked the Volkswagen bug at the very end of the jetty, surrounded by water on three sides; the bay to the left, the bar in front of him, and the Pacific Ocean to his right.

There's a storm coming in, Kirk Fletcher thought. And big waves on the horizon.

The Marriage Proposal

I
Death by Party Game
*In which Andy Peterson plays too hard and
Huck is reacquainted with mortality*

It was upon a blustery Saturday in April that an event took place which would sew the seeds of change concerning the way Huckleberry Samuel Puhzz viewed life, the universe, and his eternal bachelorhood.

He would never have guessed it from the way the day started. He'd just awakened like any other morning, hauling off to the bathroom to dispose of the previous night's beer and then dumping some Dog Chow into the bucket on the trailer's porch. The bucket was painted in nail polish with the name of Huck's hound dog, 'Whizzer,' who held the Guinness Record for 'dog sleeping the most hours consecutively.' Breakfast for Huck had been the usual mix of cold pizza, cold spaghetti, and day-old onion rings, all of which were sitting out on the kitchen counter where he'd left them so they'd be handy. You know, a traditional bachelor's morning.

The day was supposed to go normal-like too. Read the newspaper. Take a walk down to the creek with Whizzer to try and shoot the fat quail that had been eluding him all week. Back by 11:30 to watch

Wheel Of Fortune. Maybe he'd make a trip into town after three to visit Bubba at the Pump'n Munch and pick up some chew, another six-pack, and some gummi-something-or-others. Then he'd get home in time for *Touched By An Angel* or whatever else came on before Chuck Norris. It was bachelor paradise.

But, as tends to happen at the beginning of these stories, the phone rang. Huck hesitated before picking it up, seeing as how he was still dressed only in his skivvies, but then he decided to answer anyway. It was Betty Jean Essex, and she apologized for the late notice, but she wanted to invite him to a potluck party that very night.

The two of them had gotten to know each other pretty well over the past few months. Betty Jean, a spry old bird about seventy-two years of age, was in charge of Bingo & Casino Night down at the old Chinese Baptist Church. After she learned how much Huck loved the Wheel of Fortune (in an adventure which I've already recounted, so flip back a few pages if you want to know the particulars) she asked him to take over as Master Of The Casino Wheel at Bingo & Casino Night. Huck didn't care much about raising gambling money for the Chinese Baptists, but he figured the filthy lucre went to some good cause like feeding starving African children or drying out winos - and he really *really* loved that Wheel - so he accepted and helped out. He got pretty good at it too, so old Betty Jean had taken a

The Marriage Proposal

shine to him.

The potluck party was at 8:00 that evening and a lot of people Huck knew were going to be there, so he decided it would be politic for him to accept. The secret to success in life was the connections you made, and Betty Jean Essex's parties were Grand Central Station for networking in McKinleyville. The mayor would probably be there, the bank president, maybe even the manager of the Post Office. And, as a sign of the exclusivity of these get-togethers, people like Bubba and his convenience-store hangers-on would not be invited.

So, in case I haven't made myself clear, Huck said yes. Provided he didn't have to bring anything.

Some time around six he started looking for his clean clothes. Whizzer had knocked the hampers over the previous day, and in picking things up Huck had got the two mixed up and couldn't tell which were the dirty clothes and which were the clean ones, so he did a sniff test and put on his fanciest duds.

He clambered out of the trailer and started the truck at six-thirty, even though Betty Jean's was only twenty minutes away, because you never knew how many attempts it was going to take to start the damn thing. It was more comfortable than usual to drive the truck, because Grandma's shotgun was absent from the gun rack that blocked the rear window. Usually the gun whacked him on the head at least four times between home and town, but he'd lost it in the woods the day before when he threw it at the damn fat quail. Of course, he'd find it tomorrow, and then... oh, then that quail was gonna meet his maker. And on a Sunday too.

Huck parked about a block from Betty Jean's neat little yellow two-story house and walked slowly up the sidewalk, dragging his feet so that he wouldn't be too early. As luck would have it Andy Peterson, whose truck started even less often than Huck's, was dragging his feet from the other direction and they stopped in front of Betty Jean's and had a talk.

Andy Peterson had moved to McKinleyville from Centerton back in '82. The mill there was shut down (temporarily, they said, while the corporation that ran it concentrated on opening a new one in Nogales, Mexico.) Andy came to work at the one in McKinleyville, which was still in operation only because the one in Japan had become too costly to operate... something about high employee wages. Huck had met Andy while working there, but ever since Huck had thrown out his back pulling chain he'd spent most days at home on disability, mending, so these days he and Andy didn't get anywhere near enough time to chew the fat.

Today they started talking about a range of subjects. "Windy day," one said, and "Yup, blew a tree down 'cross town I heard," the other said. "Gonna storm," one suggested. "Might be thunder and lightning coming," the other responded. "Pretty wet this year," one pointed out. "Probably flood the

The Marriage Proposal

golf course again," the other predicted. "Must be El Niño," the first guessed. But then the conversation entered dangerous territory for guy-talk.

"Been seein' anybody?" Andy asked.

At first Huck wasn't sure what he meant. "You mean women?"

"Yup," Andy said.

"Not recently," Huck almost admitted, but instead he said, "Shucks, yeah."

"Good for you," Andy said. "I'm going to the Singles Dance at the Four-Square next week. I figure I gotta meet somebody soon. Hell, I'm forty-two. Don't want to die single."

"Windy day," Huck pointed out. Andy sighed and looked at his shoes for a moment.

"Yup, more trees might blow down."

When the first guests arrived Huck and Andy were rescued and they joined them at the front door. A smiling Betty Jean admitted them.

Now, I could describe the party... the colorful buffet table (a fine range of food including thirteen different guests' variations on potato salad)... what the Mayor was wearing... how high Sheriff Kearney was when he stopped by to say hello... even the details of the conversation in which Celia Mongelli tried to explain to Betty Jean Essex why Pork was not "the other white meat"...

I could describe it. But I won't.

I'll just fast forward to the event that was to

going to change the way Huck Puhzz thought about his life.

At about eight-thirty Lolondra Hawks suggested a game. The recently widowed Mayor Fletcher wanted to play charades (an idea seconded by foremost-man-of-letters Bob Thalia), but Barry Berelman, the bank president, hated them. The local catholic priest, Thaddeus Mother, wanted to guess the names of the books of the Bible and just about everybody hated that idea. It wasn't until Karen Fucchman, the librarian, suggested the game she had brought with her that there was consensus. It was Twister™, and those who wished to participate began removing their shoes.

Once their shoes were removed and the *eau du sock* began to waft around the room the guests liked the game about as much as guessing the books of the Bible, but the die was already cast and they shut up and some decided to help clean up in the kitchen. Karen Fucchman spread the big vinyl sheet with the colored circles on the living room floor and Lolondra Hawks spun the little needle on the colored wheel. The first player, Andy Peterson, placed his stocking-clad foot on the green circle and the game began.

It started out okay. Once the four players involved in the first round were all on the vinyl the contortions began. Tim Watley got a good view of Karen Fucchman's backside as she put her left hand on a red circle, and Andy Peterson had to huff and

The Marriage Proposal

puff and stretch quite a bit to slither under Jackie Hill's crotch to reach a yellow circle with his right hand. In fact, Huck noticed, Andy was huffing and puffing quite a bit.

The pile of humanity became precarious when Tim Watley was forced to slide his right foot back to a blue circle, a move that made Jackie Hill lay practically prone on the vinyl and forced Andy Peterson to arch his back like the London Bridge. The entire maze of limbs began to wobble and then Karen Fucchman called out "Shit!" and the four bodies fell into each other like collapsing dominos. The spectators roared laughter in appreciation, even though they knew their turns were coming next.

It took a few minutes, during which the players fought to extricate themselves, before anyone noticed that Andy Peterson wasn't moving. Tim called out, "Hey, Andy!" but when he got no response he looked fearfully at the crowd. There was no doctor in attendance so Barry Berelman, the only guest with proper CPR training (Sheriff Kearney, whom one might presume was educated in such matters, had left by this time) did his best to resuscitate him. Betty Jean Essex called 9-1-1 for an ambulance. But it was clear to everyone that it was too late.

Andy Peterson had died in a tragic, senseless party game accident.

Before you get too teary-eyed, just remember that this story is not about Andy Peterson. It's about Huck Puhzz. And Huck was standing in Betty Jean

Essex's living room, staring at the corpse of Andy Peterson (silhouetted, as it was, by blue, green, yellow, and red vinyl circles), thinking just one thing: "Hell, I'm forty-two. Don't want to die single."

Yes, the point to all this is that Huck's mortality had been thrust before him. He felt the years before him contract to days, he saw the days contract to hours, he saw himself scrambling on his own grave like that Scrooge fella, trying to wipe his name off that dreadful stone. Death was right around the corner, and he was running out of time. And worse, he was all alone. New ground had to be broken! He had to make changes in his life. Huck had to do some thinking about this mortality and bachelorhood problem. And for the next few weeks he actually thought about it. Of course, he strenuously avoided coming to any conclusions. And by May he'd conveniently forgotten it all.

II
The Best Supporting Actress Comes To Humboldt County
In which the most gorgeous creature on Earth comes to Ferndale

It was early May when Huck Puhzz stood gawking at the poster in the Food Mart window.

You couldn't throw a dead cat in

The Marriage Proposal

McKinleyville that spring without hitting one of them. The shiny orange posters hung in every single store, restaurant, and office window in the city, advertising the Grand Reopening of the Redwood Area Theatre Society's community theatre in Ferndale. There was so much orange around the town that some people figured Halloween had come early. So if you didn't show up on opening night there was no way you could say it was because you hadn't seen the publicity.

The Fuller Brush Theatre, as it was officially known, was built in 1844 by, of course, Fuller Brush (an individual, not to be confused with the broom company of the same name.) The Theatre was a magnificent three-story victorian structure with bay windows in the lobby and towers at each corner. Fuller had been the kind of guy who hated waste in any form and, as part-owner of the Southern Humboldt Timber Company, felt it was necessary to use every piece of scrap wood, wood shaving, and irregularly cut lumber that his company created. The result was that he built dozens upon dozens of buildings, even though most were not needed for any specific purpose, and he covered them with layers upon layers of decorative molding carved from this waste wood. By the time of his death in 1867 he had created a town of sixty-three buildings which were occupied only by the dozen or so construction workers who were living in them and working hard building still more.

And each and every one of these buildings was weighed down with tons of the victorian molding decorations that architects called "gingerbread."

After Fuller's death the buildings spent several years as a ghost town, and then the Southern Humboldt Timber Company began lodging its employees in them. Because "Southern Humboldt Timber Company Worker Housing" was an unfriendly moniker they had a dedication and christened the community "The Village Of Ferndale," which was much warmer and homier. Eventually times began to change and, after a few decades passed, the nearby forests were mostly cut down and the Timber Company decided to relocate to Oregon. But by then (luckily for the village's merchants) tourists had discovered the unique and quaint collection of victorian edifices. The village became an assortment of antique shops, arts and crafts galleries, used book stores, a few restaurants, and a very nice chocolate shop. And in the center of all of these quaint and souvenir-friendly businesses was the Fuller Brush Theatre.

Unfortunately the Theatre was severely damaged in "The Big One" of 1990. As Californians know, every region of California has its own earthquake referred to as "The Big One." When you're new to an area you always have to ask, "So, when was 'The Big One' around here?" In San Francisco, for instance, despite numerous earthquakes in the years since, the 1906 shake is still "The Big One." In Ferndale "The Big One" was the 6.2 shaker that

The Marriage Proposal

knocked about a quarter of downtown off its foundations in 1990. The good folks of RATS had dedicated themselves to raising money to refurbish the theatre so that they could give performances there (mostly on weekends when tourists from the big city come visiting with their money.)

The success or failure of the Grand Opening fundraiser for the Fuller Brush Theatre was riding on the fact that Lolondra Hawks, chairman of the financial committee for RATS, had invited an "old friend" she'd gone to grammar school in San Francisco with to speak at the ceremony, an actress named Felecia Vandermark. Ms. Vandermark, as everyone learned thanks to the bright orange posters, was a former Academy Award™ nominee. And it was Ms. Vandermark's visit that started Huck Puhzz down a dangerous new road.

First, a few notes about Ms. Felecia Vandermark;

Back in 1985, after a long, uneven career in soap operas (alternating annually between being a heroine and a vixen), Felecia was accidentally sent an audition invitation by her agent that was meant for another client. She attended the audition and was cast in a very low-budget independent movie directed by an up-and-coming young fellow who had just graduated from the USC film school. The resulting film, *"Six Bank Robbers In Albuquerque,"* was a black & white crime drama shot on 16mm that got virtually no attention in the United States. It did, however, became a favorite of the French at that year's Cannes Film Festival (a fact which speaks volumes about the film itself.) The movie received several Academy Award™ nominations, possibly because of the cachét from this foreign attention. (You'll have to look cachét up in the dictionary. Huck did.) What's more, Felecia was somehow nominated for best supporting actress, probably because the Academy members felt sorry for her since she'd already lost the Soap Opera Daytime Best Vixen Emmy Award™ fourteen times in a row. Of course when the Oscars™ were handed out she lost there too, but by now she was very good at losing and maintaining a camera-ready plastic smile. That's acting.

"Just being nominated is honor enough," she told reporters for the fifteenth time.

Her career, since that momentary blip, had been a complete bust, unfortunately. Even the soap opera job dried up when the producers fired her to make room for a younger actress who had quit life as a bouncing *Bayguard* in order to "stretch her abilities." The wasteland years had been hard on her ego, but once you've been nominated for an Oscar™, well, you always have that small piece of immortality to cling to, and Felecia damn well used it at every occasion.

Thus the largest words on the RATS Ferndale Theatre Grand Reopening poster weren't the Theatre's name or the date or time of the first show or even what the first show was going to be. They

The Marriage Proposal

were: SPECIAL GUEST - FELECIA VANDERMARK, NOMINATED FOR AN ACADEMY AWARD™ FOR BEST SUPPORTING ACTRESS, 1986. In Hollywood, Felecia Vandermark was already long forgotten, considered a has-been at 41. But in Humboldt County she was still royalty.

So, as I already pointed out, Huck Puhzz was gawking at the poster in the Food Mart window. He'd never seen *"Six Bank Robbers In Albuquerque"* because it was black & white and artsy and he didn't understand that sort of thing. But he had seen Felecia Vandermark many many times when, after *Wheel Of Fortune* was over, he'd switched channels to watch *The Young & The Children*. There, every weekday in full color, her peroxide blond locks flowing and clad in the latest designer clothing, Felecia had lived the tragic soap opera life of Sally St. Cloud, nurse at People's Hospital. In fact, some days he thought she was even finer than Vanna White, which in Huck's world was akin to heresy. To him Felecia Vandermark was a vision.

It didn't make any difference to Huck what play would be performed on the theatre's stage or what festivities would take place at the Grand Opening ceremonies. All he cared about was getting a chance to see her, Felecia Vandermark, in the glorious flesh. That he would be able to stand before her with only air between his eyes and hers. That he could hear her voice live, unsullied by microphones and poor recordings. That he could see the real thing.

As you might guess, Huck didn't stand gawking at the poster for long. He was the very first person to buy a ticket for the Grand Reopening at Shafer's Hardware. And when the Grand Reopening day came he was the very first person in line for the cheap seats.

He almost got a glimpse of the Best Supporting Actress Nominee of 1986 when she arrived at the theatre on Ferndale's horse-drawn carriage (used on weekends by the aforementioned tourists.) Unfortunately there was too big a crowd and so he had to muscle his way into the theatre and wait for a good look with everyone else.

Huck wasn't a religious man, per se, but he believed that if angels existed they would probably be tall, slim, blonde, blue-eyed, and move with the grace of a girl who had spent six years in the Little Miss Professional Finishing School. When Felecia Vandermark finally came out before the audience she was, in Huck's eyes, all that and more. She glided out onto that stage like ball bearings in fresh 10-40 weight, and when she spoke it was more melodious than Hootie & The Blowfish.

"Thank you for inviting me to this opening, and thank you for patronizing this wonderful theatre," she said. "It will be a magnet for the arts on the North Coast and bring still more renown to this

The Marriage Proposal

beautiful redwood region. I hope you enjoy the play."

And that was it. She went and sat down and the play started. Huck figured that fifteen bucks was a bit steep for forty-four words (counting the 'and's and 'the's), but he got to look at her too. He sat there, catching a glimpse of her hair above the audience, and stood on his seat after the play to get a good view of her as she exited.

When Huck got home the glowing image of the Best Supporting Actress Nominee remained in his mind's eye (a myopic thing at best) and he described her in angelic detail to Whizzer as he fried them up a couple of pork chops. But he didn't think about Felecia Vandermark really seriously until the next day when his world was shattered by his brother's terrifying news.

III
The Decline & Sudden Fall Of Bubba Puhzz
In which Bubba takes a crash course in love

As the sun set, the shadows slowly crawled up the walls of the Pump'n Munch Convenience Store & Gas Mart until any part of the building's exterior not directly illuminated by the cheap flickering fluorescent parking lights had been plunged into an unholy darkness. Huck hiked up his Levis and dashed into the brightly lit interior of the store, but given the events about to transpire he might just as well have remained in the creeping blackness outside. There was no full moon but, as Huck would soon come to realize, there was certainly lunacy afoot.

The posse; Sammy, Hampton, Big Kenny, Larry, and Little Larry, had assembled in the store shortly after Bubba took over his night manager shift (as usual.) Huck was planning to tell them about his encounter with the Best Supporting Actress Nominee of 1986, but his brother spoke up first.

"Met a girl last night," Bubba said. "Met her at my line dancing class." He passed around some beers courtesy of Truman Krantz, the store's generous owner (although Mr. Krantz wasn't aware of his generosity, and if he had been Bubba would have quickly become an ex-night manager.)

"What kind of place is that to meet someone?" Huck huffed. He was just a bit peeved that Bubba had beaten him to the first story.

"It's a place. Where do you find your dates?" Bubba asked, poking Huck in the chest with a wet Michelob.

Hampton smiled conspiratorially. "I get my dates through the 'Fish Phone.'"

"The Fish Phone?!" Big Kenny said, dropping his copy of Heavy Metal magazine. "What're you looking for, Hamp? Women or fish?"

"That's disgusting," Sammy added.

Hampton became defensive. "Hey, the Fish

The Marriage Proposal

Phone is run by this guy who owns Pappy's Sporting Goods. You call up the number and the recording gives you pretty good fishing information. But if you're a paying member and you type in your secret member code on your touch-tone phone you get a different recording that tells you which women have recently become single. You know, broke up with their boyfriends, got divorced, got widowed..."

"They should leave Mayor Fletcher on there permanently," Larry pointed out.

"Sounds pretty desperate when you get leads on your love life from an old fisherman whose idea of a good Friday night is staying home tying flies."

"Well, I had three dates last month," Hampton pointed out, "so don't knock it until you've tried it."

"Met a girl last night," Bubba repeated, looking down at the greasy floor and shuffling a bit. "Name's Cheryl. Pretty nice girl."

The posse went quiet. I mean, it was so quiet you could have heard a mouse fart. These were very unusual adjectives coming from their leader's mouth. "Great boobs" was okay Saturday night fare. "Legs from the Earth to the Moon" was one of Sammy's favorites. "I wouldn't throw her out of bed for eatin' crackers" was a staple. Sometimes, if it was late enough and they'd had enough beer, they got as crass and lewd as most men usually get when it's late enough and they've had enough beer. But "pretty nice girl" was definitely not part of the usual vocabulary.

"You getting sweet on some line-dancing tramp you just met last night?" Big Kenny laughed. He stopped laughing as Bubba turned quickly and grabbed him by the front collar with one hand and raised his other hand clenched in a fist. A dangerous move considering Kenny was twice his size. Everyone was still and (gasp) sober now. Bubba was not known for being a physical person. "What did I say?" Big Kenny asked. "What?"

"Don't you ever talk that way again about the girl I'm going to marry," Bubba said. I'm not sure, but I think a pin dropped.

"Say what?" Sammy mumbled.

"I asked Cheryl to marry me this morning. We're gettin' married in six weeks," Bubba said.

You see, Bubba had been struck by cupid's arrow, and the humors of his passion had arisen out of balance to all others and from their foam arose the embodiment of his adoration not unlike Aphrodite arising from the sea. Or, to put it in plain English, he fell head over heels in love at first sight with Miss Cheryl Wingate almost as soon as he spied her rocking and stomping to "Achy Breaky Heart."

It had started out just like any other Friday night, dumping off the posse on his way home and then sneaking back to The Country Club to take line-dancing lessons at midnight. (If the guys had known they would have chewed and teased him mercilessly.) He hadn't even had four beers when he

The Marriage Proposal

saw her, bouncing along like a sweet whirling dervish on an assembly line. In the first five minutes he had known that she was his destiny, even before he waylaid her coming off the dance floor and introduced himself.

"My beautiful dear, my name is Bubba Puhzz, and I am madly and deeply in love with you," he'd said.

"Natch," she'd said, and they'd sat down to have beers.

To cut to the chase, Bubba didn't go home that night, and the next morning he was engaged to be married. He figured it had taken him eight years to get promoted from stock room clerk at the Pump'n Munch to his now lofty position as Night Manager, and he wasn't going to let his romantic life drag along at the same stultifying rate. Sometimes when you knew what you wanted you just had to reach out and take it.

"In six weeks?" Hampton asked. "Isn't that a bit fast, Bubba?"

"Why wait?" Bubba said, turning around to busy himself at the donut cabinet.

"You just met her twenty hours ago, you dolt! Are you out of your mind?!" Huck growled. No foolin', he actually growled.

Of course, although it might have been prudent for Bubba to get to know the lady in question a bit more that wasn't really the part of all this that was sticking in Huck's craw so bad. It was that Bubba had beat him to it again. Bubba had always had the better grades (a C+ average!) and he had a whole posse of friends to make trouble with instead of just that turncoat Hunsey Bourcarte. Bubba always got the better jobs and usually made more money and got all that free beer. Bubba had always been Momma's favorite. Now he had a line-dancing wife too. What did Huck have? He had a broken-down trailer, a hound dog good only at sleeping, and a monthly disability check.

Damn, if life wasn't unfair.

"I want you to be my best man, Larry," Bubba said.

Damn, if life wasn't really, really unfair.

"What about me?" Huck demanded.

"You're an usher. You gotta carry Momma."

Well, that about broke the camel's back. Huck got off his stool and set down his free beer and then stomped off toward the door.

"I'm gonna be busy in six weeks," he said loudly, and he made sure that he slammed the door as hard as he could (although it just swung through the other direction silently and then came to rest.)

Beating this one was going to take every bit of his ingenuity (if such could be located). Sabotaging Bubba's matrimonial bliss would be too mean-spirited, even for Huck. No, he had to beat Bubba fair and square on the field of one-upmanship. There was only one possible solution.

He had to find a bride and arrange for a wedding ceremony in less than six weeks.

It would solve more than one problem. Ever since poor Andy Peterson's tragic death the month before, Huck had been concerned about his own mortality and, especially, the prospect of dying alone. A man his age was supposed to have a wife, for Chrissake. You weren't supposed to be a bachelor at forty-two.

Instead of going directly to his car, Huck started walking downtown. He found that he thought better when he was moving (more oxygen to his brain cells.) No ideas came and went as he walked, no brilliant plans formed as he marched past the storefronts in frustration.

And then a brilliant orange poster, left posted in the window by the absent-minded owner of J.J.'s Bookstore, caught his eye and everything fell into place.

IV
The Marriage Proposal
In which Huck matches all bets

Huck Puhzz had always been number two after his brother Bubba. In school he was just another one of the kids who wouldn't graduate from High School. As an adult he was just another manual laborer. As a friend he was just a hanger-on who didn't have any money and survived on his disability checks. He had absolutely no skills whatsoever. So it was natural that women, in general, didn't usually perceive him as a "good catch."

Of course, Huck saw things from a different perspective.

And now he saw that the answer to all of his problems was simple.

It took him a while, rummaging through the dark and grimy corners of his trailer, to find a piece of paper or a pen. He wasn't in the habit of writing things down. Phone numbers were kept on the chalkboard next to his refrigerator. He paid his power and telephone bills in cash at the offices in town, so he rarely wrote checks. When he was required to contact Momma, due to a holiday or special event, he called her on the telephone. In fact, he had to think for a few minutes about whether or not he actually owned a pen or pencil.

Huck finally located what he needed and sat down at the kitchen counter, clearing away the four-day old pizza. With his day-glo Bic Click in hand and a piece of blank onionskin paper he'd found separating two snapshots in Gramma's photo album in front of him, he began to compose his letter. The words flowed easily because they came from his heart. Of course, he also felt the spectre of brother Bubba's impending nuptials looming large above him. This letter was going to be the brilliant masterstroke that would hand Huck a crushing victory in a sibling war that had lasted more than thirty years.

He printed to make it especially legible.

Dear Miss Vandermark,

My name is Huckleberry Samuel Puhzz. My brother's friends call me Huck. I live in Humboldt County where you visited last week to open the big theater. When I saw you on that stage I just fell in love. I also fell in love with you when I saw you cheating on Ronaldo on your TV show. Now, I know you're a big movie star and all, and probably get calls from Brad Pitt and Burt Reynolds every day, but those boys in Hollywood are all druggies and just want a pretty teenager on their arm, not a regular woman. But me, I'm different. I'm looking for a older lady who is still beautiful but has been around the block a few times. I think you're just that lady.

I don't expect you to go hog wild about me just because I said I love you, so here are my vital statistics; I was born and grew up in Humboldt County. My Daddy worked on the railroad and was killed one night when he leaned out the side of the caboose too far to dunk some tobacco spit and got clipped by a light pole. My Momma cleaned the house until she got too infirm and now she's laid up at the convalescent home. I have a brother named Bubba who is the night manager at the Pump'n Munch Convenience Store & Gas Mart and a step-sister who ran away with a carousel operator when she was twelve because women are mostly no good. Not you, of course. You're as right as rain.

I did good in grammar school and made it all the way to the tenth grade, when me and my best friend, that traitor Hunsey, quit to become real men and work at the mill. I was a hard worker and I always paid for dinner when I went out on a date - none of that letting the girl pay sometimes or that weird European Dutch paying.

I have my own Airstream that I live in, bought and paid for, on an acre I bought with my Daddy's insurance money. My loyal hound dog, Whizzer, and I live here and watch your show every day - seeing as how I'm on disability 'cause of my bad back and am home when your show comes on. I even think you're more beautiful than Vanna White.

So I figure that I love you more than anybody else on earth and would treat you really special so here goes: Will you marry me?

My Love, Your Future Husband (I hope)
Huck Puhzz

P.S. Could you answer as quick as you can? It would be really good if you said yes and we got married in less than six weeks, because my brother is getting married in six weeks and it would be bad if we got married on the same weekend since his friends are coming to my wedding too.

Huck had gotten the address of Felecia Vandermark's agent and publicist from Lolondra Hawks, and he scrawled this between the lines of his own scratched-out address on the recycled gas bill envelope he had prepared. Four double-licked ten-cent stamps later Huck was out the door, leaping over Whizzer in a single bound. He had twenty minutes until the post office closed for the day (looking for that pen and paper had taken longer than he'd expected.)

A plan for the evening began to form in his mind (there was plenty of room for it.) After mailing his letter he would go directly to the Pump'n Munch. Bubba and his posse would be forming and he would drop the bombshell on them, explain that he had also proposed marriage. But not to some simple line-dancing wench, oh no, he had proposed to the Best Supporting Actress Nominee for 1986. He had proposed to Hollywood royalty, someone with class and fame, maybe even with money (although, Huck reminded his conscience, he would never marry for money. He loved her.)

Once the posse was sufficiently impressed he would trek on over to the Eureka-I-Found-It Coffee

Shop, where Alverna Kettle, McKinleyville's resident gossip-monger and teller-of-tales, would surely be dining. If he told her about his proposal, well, by tomorrow everyone in town would know. He'd be famous. People would want to be him. People would want to shake his hand and they'd beg for autographs. Maybe the town would have an annual Huck and Felecia Day. And Bubba, he would be absolutely green. Victory would belong to Huck.

Huck got to the post office in time but arrived at the Pump'n Munch a bit too early. Big Kenny was seated at one end of the bench in front of the store, and Hampton and Sammy were planted on the other end, as usual, for ballast. Tonight the three of them were having a heated debate about the best location of the rabbit-ears for indoor television reception. The gas pump fumes would soon get the better of them and then they'd head on in for cheese twists. Larry and his son Little Larry were still at work, but would be arriving any minute, heeding the call of free beer. Huck loitered near the air & water station and then headed in.

"I proposed," Huck told them when they'd all assembled.

"Proposed what?" Sammy asked. Big Kenny and Hampton were flipping through a local tabloid going over listings of strippers for Bubba's bachelor party and they didn't even bother to look up.

"Proposed marriage, you thick-head! What else?" Huck said in exasperation. "I'm getting mar-

The Marriage Proposal

ried!" Only Larry responded.

"To who?" he asked.

"Miss Felecia Vandermark," Huck answered proudly. Again, only Larry looked up. Bubba was washing the counter, but he did slow up a bit.

"Was she the one that used to run the old slushy stand in Centerton?" Larry asked. "She always made a fine slushy."

"No! For God's sake, don't you guys have any culture?! Miss Felecia Vandermark was the Best Supporting Actress Nominee for 1986! She's a movie star!"

"Was she the one in *'Forrest Gump'?*" Hampton asked. "I saw *'Forrest Gump.'* That lady was pretty good looking until she was supposed to be all drugged up and strung out and then she looked like a - "

"No, she wasn't in *'Forrest Gump!'*" Huck said. Now the entire posse, Bubba included, was looking up at him.

"What was she in?" Sammy asked. Huck thought about this one for a minute, because he couldn't quite remember the title of *"Six Bank Robbers In Albuquerque."* He gave it his best shot.

"*'Killers In Santa Fe,'* " he said.

"I saw that," Hampton ventured.

"What else?" Sammy asked. Okay, Huck was stuck on that one. He didn't know if Felecia Vandermark had ever done another movie. So he fessed up.

"She plays Miss Sally St. Cloud on *The Young & The Children,*' " he admitted. Now recognition dawned in the posse's faces, although few of them would have admitted to ever watching a soap opera. There was a pause as they all thought this one through. Finally, Larry stood up and approached Huck, stopping when they were almost face-to-face.

"And she said yes?" he asked, incredulous.

Suddenly the temperature dropped about ten degrees for poor Huck.

Not once since he had conceived of his brilliant plan had it ever occurred to him that Miss Felecia Vandermark might say no. Not once had he considered the many ways in which his proposal could, if turned down, make his standing in the town, in the posse, and in relation to his brother, infinitely worse. Now all these unthunk thoughts came raining down on him like hailstones (you know, like those golf-ball-sized hailstones) and he started to shift from one foot to the other. His face grew pale. His bowels grew weak.

"Not yet," he said tremulously.

"Exactly when did you talk to her and propose?" Larry asked.

"I just mailed it," Huck said slowly. "To her agent," he added, regretting it immediately.

Well, there was a split-second of silence and then the boys broke out in the best laugh they'd had in about six months. Beer came out of Hampton's nose in little squirts. Big Kenny had been eatin' a

The Marriage Proposal

corn dog and started to choke and turned red, but Sammy gave him a quick Heimlich, laughing himself the whole time. Bubba didn't laugh quite so hard, but he had a cheshire-cat grin on his face and was shakin his head.

Huck stood mortified.

"You'll see!" Huck said, backing toward the door. "She is going to say yes! I am going to marry a Hollywood movie star! All her big Hollywood friends'll be at the wedding - and just for this, I ain't going to invite any of you!"

Needless to say, Huck did not go by the Eureka!-I-Found-It Coffee Shop that night to tell Alverna Kettle about his marriage proposal.

But by noon the next day the entire town had heard about it anyway.

V
Twenty-Two Days Of The Dog
In which the ante is raised

Within twenty-four hours of the moment when Huck Puhzz mailed his marriage proposal to the Best Supporting Actress Nominee for 1986 everyone in McKinleyville knew about it. Since brother Bubba's impending wedding to Miss Cheryl Wingate of McKinleyville had been announced in the 'Community News' section of the Centerton *Post-Standard* the very same day it seemed obvious to most of the town's citizens that Huck's move was a desperate and pathetic attempt to call his brother's bet by tossing an engagement of his own into the pot.

And the citizens were exactly right.

As a side effect there was also quite a run at the library on any old copies of The National Muckraker which featured salacious sex scandals and tawdry tales of yo-yo dieting involving Miss Felecia Vandermark, the aforementioned nominee.

But despite the apparent hopelessness of the situation, Huck wasn't about to give up.

So Huck did everything he could to prepare for a positive outcome. The new mailbox he quickly installed at the end of his driveway was so polished you could see the sun reflecting from it two miles down Highway 52. Every day, the minute that the mail truck pulled up (unless *Wheel Of Fortune* or *The Young & The Children* were on), Huck jogged out to the new mailbox and checked to see if his distinguished fiancée-to-be had written to him with her answer. Even his hound dog Whizzer took to sleeping next to the mailbox out at the road instead of his favorite place underneath the trailer.

Huck stopped going to the Pump'n Munch for beers and had the grocery store deliver his food, just in case a Federal Express or RPS truck came by with an overnight letter from his true love. Larry took his check into the bank every Friday for him and cashed it in (for a slight fee) so he wouldn't miss

The Marriage Proposal

a phone call or a telegram. In fact, Huck became housebound (or mailbox-bound). But the first week dragged by and there was nothing. And the second week certainly wasn't any better.

The month wore on, and every day Huck made the walk up to the mailbox, but every day he found the same; bills, jury summons, and notifications that he may already have won something. The posse started to talk, then Alverna Kettle started to talk, and pretty soon everybody in town started to talk. Huck Puhzz had lost his mind.

Larry tried, on one of his bank runs, to get Huck involved in planning Bubba's bachelor party. The posse had rented the Elks' Hall for a night and the Pump'n Munch's franchise owner, Truman Krantz, had offered to donate the booze (which he probably would have done anyway, whether he knew it or not.) It was going to be an all-guy deal, like bachelor parties are supposed to be. But, better yet, there wasn't even a chance that the women would come a-spying, because they were going to be busy having a bridal shower for Cheryl over at the Chinese Baptist Church the same night. The whole subject only angered Huck, and he threw Larry out and told him he'd find somebody else to get his money.

Huck, to be honest, felt kind of trapped at this point. Sibling rivalry or no, he wanted to be at his brother's bachelor party (at the very least to see the strippers) and he wanted to usher at his brother's wedding. But he'd dug himself an unfortunate hole with this proposal thing and admitting it was only going to put him into it even deeper. So he just shut up and watched the mailbox.

The thing that bothered Huck the most during this time was the absence so far of any jeers, scorn, mockery, and general meanspirited teasing from Bubba and the posse. When Huck had been pulling down eight bills a month at the mill he'd teased Bubba unmercifully about his meager pay at the Pump'n Munch. Then, when Huck had been put on disability and Bubba had gotten his promotion to night manager, well, Bubba had turned the tables something fierce. It was tradition. Now Bubba and the boys had a perfect opportunity to give it to him but good. "What kind of Hollywood star is going to give you two looks, trailer trash?" they could be saying. "Of course, you have sooo much to offer a girl." "Heard you were having an affair with the mailman, Huck." "I seen that movie star you're in love with, Huck, isn't she named Rosie Palm?" "That hound dog startin' to look good to you, Huck?" "Hold it, Huck! I think hell is freezing over!" But they didn't say a word. Not one. It was almost spooky.

Bubba called twice just to update Huck on the wedding plans, and he was nice about it to boot. Fact of the matter was, Bubba had never cared much for the whole sibling battle anyway. He'd always played along just because Huck did it and he figured that Huck enjoyed it in some twisted way. Back when they were boys, after Pop had got whacked and

The Marriage Proposal

Momma started to go a little frayed around the edges, the two of them had sorta been on their own. Bubba, as the oldest (by nine months) had become man of the house, which Huck resented to no end (after all, what's nine months?) That was when the war had started, Bubba supposed. Four police calls and two small kitchen fires later they'd gotten old enough to move out into their own places. But it hadn't cooled down the rivalry one iota.

The third week began to pass, and still no letter.

Hampton stopped by once to return Huck's welder (which he'd borrowed more than a year ago) and stayed to watch *Walker, Texas Ranger* with him. Larry, who'd continued to cash Huck's checks, only talked about the bachelor party and asked about that annoying quail from the ravine out back that Huck could never seem to shoot.

Horsefeathers Snoqualmie, Huck's one-time almost sweetheart (all six-foot-four of her) called and in a concerned voice asked Huck if he'd like her to bring by some emu eggs for his breakfasts. He said no, he wasn't hungry.

"You aren't going to do something foolish if she doesn't write back?" Horsefeathers asked him.

"Probably not," he replied and then listlessly hung up without remembering to say goodbye to her. He didn't even stop to reflect on that little peek of fishnet stocking between the bottom of Horsefeathers' long black dress and her hightop boots that he'd always found so appealing. The depression was beginning to ruin what little was left of his mind. Why didn't Felecia write back? How many better offers was she getting?

One day there was a knock at the trailer door and Huck thought that maybe it was the mailman with a special delivery at long last. But it was just Andy and Merry Cunningham and their four-year-old, Logan, who Huck referred to as the mud-child because mud seemed to be the boy's favorite place to play. The young couple lived in a big shiny silver trailer on a two-acre lot up the road from Huck. The trailer was their "temporary residence" while they were building their "dream house," and it had been so for seven years. A year or two back the foundation of the new house had finally been poured (creating a wonderfully huge mud-box for the mud-child) but the rest of the house remained "in-progress." Huck figured they'd probably finish the place just in time to sell it and move into a retirement home.

Merry had heard that he was feelin' blue and made some preserves from the blackberries that grew on the weedy vines which threatened to take over the entire countryside. "Really sweet this year," Merry told him with a smile. "Really tart," Andy said. "Hope your actress lady says yes," Merry comforted him. "Aw, you're better off without her," Andy countered. "See you tomorrow," Merry said. "We're going to be gone for a week," Andy contradicted. Word had it that this regular difference of

The Marriage Proposal

opinion was why their house remained unbuilt. Freeman Floor Planning had already run off more than 133 different house blueprints for the Cunninghams (who were their favorite customers.)

Huck thanked them politely, but inwardly he seethed. Why was everybody being so damn nice to him? He wasn't going to have this town feeling sorry for him. They just didn't seem to understand. He was going to come out of this alright, because she was gonna say yes.

Of course, he ate the preserves.

Even as self-assured as Huck had convinced himself to be, he was still a bit startled when, on the twenty-second day of his seclusion, the mailman left an envelope in his box that wasn't a bill, an ad, or another offer from a long-distance phone company. Suspicious, he'd examined the letter very closely. It was just a regular everyday white envelope, size ten, with his name and address written on its front in looping script. There was no return address, just a name written in the top left corner.

Felecia Vandermark.

"It took him a few minutes to lock up the mobile home because the blocks it sat on had shifted and the door didn't close so well anymore. He got down on all fours and peered under the deck to see if he could make out Whizzer in case the aging mutt wanted to go to town too, but the unmoving lump in the dark under the back of the mobile didn't respond to his calls and whistles."
   page 7

VI
A Letter Arrives
In which Huck receives an answer to his question

When Huck Puhzz received his soon-to-be-famous letter from Miss Felecia Vandermark, Best Supporting Actress Nominee for 1986, he wasn't sure what to do first. Should he open it and read it? Or should he drive on into town and tell all those Doubting Thomases and unbelievers who'd said he was crazy that - HA HAH! - he'd actually received it?! Those twenty-two days waiting by the mailbox were going to be worth it when he saw their jaws drop.

But then again, what if she'd turned him down? What if this envelope contained nothing more than further embarrassment and ridicule? Maybe he should read it before bragging about it this time.

In the end he thought ahead (a first time occurrence) and decided to open it first.

The letter was written by hand, in the same looping cursive that had addressed the envelope. The paper was ivory-colored and textured, with little pieces of paper fuzz along its deliberately tattered edges. He reminded himself that he'd have to frame the letter (and the envelope) at a later date. His heart began to beat madly in his chest as he read the contents.

Dear Mister Huckleberry Samuel Puhzz,
    I am honored to receive your proposal of

marriage. You seem a kind and considerate man. I'm afraid I cannot accommodate your six-week timetable for being wed, however. I have always believed that two people must get to know each other adequately before they can begin conjugal relations. The state of matrimony is to be entered into only by two adults who have reflected upon one another and evaluated each other completely.

That does not mean, however, that I reject your proposal out of hand, so do not despair! I suggest that we continue our correspondence and over time get to know more about each other's interests and personalities. If these letters suggest a series of mutual interests then we can arrange at some future time a face to face meeting in order to continue our courtship. So that we may keep our communications discreet, please mail all future letters to Mail Services, Etc., P.O. Box 6694, Centerton, CA 95502-6694, and they will be forwarded to me. I look forward to your next missive.

    Yours sincerely,
Felecia Vandermark

Huck started over again at "Dear Mister."

After he read it through the second time, Huck paused only a moment and then started digging through the old newspapers for his dictionary.

The Marriage Proposal

Now, I'm not even going to try to fool you for a minute, because just about anybody reading this has got to be at least twice as smart as Huck Puhzz. The return address in Centerton, just five miles from Huck's front door, would be a red flag for most intelligent human beings. One of us might then take a gander at the revered envelope and check out the McKinleyville postmark that was sloppily stamped on it. To any normal person these might raise suspicions as to its origins. But, as the author was clearly already aware, those things would never occur to Huck. So Huck never questioned the authenticity of his letter, and he just translated the harder words into language he could comprehend. Then, placing both the letter and envelope in a shoebox for protection, he hurried out to the truck. It started on the third attempt and he headed into town.

To their credit, the townspeople ate a little crow. Bubba read the letter carefully, occasionally referring to Huck's simple-language cheat sheet, and then admitted to Huck that it certainly looked good for an eventual union with the Best Supporting Actress Nominee. He even congratulated him. The posse likewise was apologetic, and they all offered Huck a few of Truman Krantz's free beers. Feeling jubilant, Huck accepted at least five.

To insure maximum exposure, this time after saying goodbye to Bubba and the posse, he went by the Eureka!-I-Found-It Coffee Shop for a piece of pie and told Denise and Art all about the letter, speaking very loudly. He did this mostly so that Alverna Kettle, who was seated at a booth by the windows, could hear every word. The only reason he didn't bother to officially inform the newspapers was because he thought that a full-blown press release might go beyond Miss Vandermark's request that things be kept "discreet" (a word which, Huck had discovered, meant "having or showing good judgment and self-restraint in speech or behavior." Funny, Huck had never heard of "discreet" before.)

Within hours everyone in the county knew that Miss Felecia Vandermark had written back to Huck and that he and the Best Supporting Actress Nominee were an actual item.

Now that his honor was unbesmirched, Huck decided to be magnanimous and cooperate with Bubba's wedding plans. True, Bubba would wind up being the brother who got married first. But at least now Huck was sort of engaged at the same time, so whatever victory Bubba could squeeze out of the situation was practically meaningless. Besides, Bubba hadn't really tormented Huck at all over the past three weeks. Huck figured this was probably because his brother was so involved in his relationship with Cheryl he'd forgotten his obligations to his other relationships. But the reason didn't matter. They were, after all, family, and family is supposed to come together at times like these. So Huck decided to give the boy a break. It was almost as if a cease-fire had been called in their never-ending war, at least for the

The Marriage Proposal

duration of the matrimonial festivities. In fact, Larry assigned Huck a list of duties associated with the bachelor party, including making out the invitations, and Huck didn't mind it a bit.

Before he did that, however, there was something else he had to do. He had to respond to Miss Felecia Vandermark's letter.

Huck, as has been noted previously, was not at heart a writer. In fact, he'd only gotten one grade better than a 'D' on any essay or book report he'd ever bothered to turn in. So he just wrote out, in as clear English as he could, his entire life story, starting with the earliest moments he could remember and ending with the moment he saw Miss Felecia on the Fuller Brush Theatre's stage.

He wondered if he should include mention of all of his relations with women, including his infamous kiss with Horsefeathers Snoqualmie. Not that there were all that many women who could say they'd slept with Huck. Really, there were only a dozen or so. Maybe a few less than that. Actually, just a couple. Even fewer than that would ever admit it. But he decided that honesty was the best policy so he wrote the details of every relationship he'd ever had into his letter. For extra effect (and to prove that he was an intellectual kind of guy) he attached the aforementioned book report ("The Life Of Augustus Caesar," from Miss Gilbert's sixth grade class, with a big C- in red ink in the upper right hand corner of the front page).

When finished, the letter ran about six pages, and with the four-page book report the entire thing ran ten. Certainly the longest epistle Huck had ever manufactured. He had written the letter with a brand-new ballpoint pen on scented stationery he'd bought at Pacific Paper Company & Office Supply, and he carefully inserted the entire sheaf into an crisp new manila envelope he'd bought there too. Just to be sure, he sealed it using both the little metal hooks and the adhesive, and then addressed it to Miss Felecia's post office box in Centerton. If she wanted to know what he was interested in, then he was going to tell her. These pages represented every single thing he knew about himself. With luck she'd want to arrange that face-to-face meeting the minute she'd finished reading it.

VII
Where's Hunsey Bourcarte?
In which the greatest mystery in McKinleyville history is considered

Huck's life became complicated again when Larry, his brother's best man and bachelor party chairman, gave him the list of the people he was supposed to make out invitations for. The forty or so guys on the list included just about everyone in town who knew Bubba by name. The only problem for

The Marriage Proposal

Huck was that these were all his brother's friends. Not a single friend of Huck's was on the list.

Now, that might make sense to most of us, considering it was his brother's bachelor party and not Huck's. But Huck could imagine himself (if he thought really, really hard) sitting in a corner at the party, all alone with no one to talk to, and he didn't like it one bit. Sure, he knew all the guys in the posse, but they were only his friends by way of Bubba. He wanted a friend of his own to invite (mostly so he wouldn't seem like such a pathetic, friendless loser in front of Bubba.)

The trouble was Huck finally realized, after trying to remember who all of his friends were, that he'd only had one true childhood friend, the infamous turncoat Hunsey Bourcarte.

Hunsey Bourcarte... adults reacted in horror at the mention of his name, while the town's children held him in the kind of reverence reserved for fallen or missing-in-action heroes. After the Great McKinleynapping Hunsey had gone through a period of savage teenage delinquency which the citizens of McKinleyville still spoke about to this day (the tale of which I shall tell you after you are privy to the important information below), and then he had turned his back on Huck and Humboldt County. Without so much as a by-your-leave Hunsey had moved on to the "Big City."

Reports of his activities there diminished over the years. There were a few reliable stories that

Hunsey had broken up with his equally notorious girlfriend. One frequently honest source said Hunsey had joined the Marines, which encouraged those who believed he could be rehabilitated, but most people didn't buy it. After a few years even Alverna Kettle didn't have much new information. Of course, people still told the sort of myths and legends which always grow after a figure as colorful as Hunsey vanishes into the ether of distant cities and lands.

Some folks said he had become a serial killer and murdered thirty-two coeds after tattooing their breasts with pictures of Gumby and Pokey. Others claimed he had become a hit man for the CIA and was responsible for killing Sonny Bono. One wild tale said he'd moved to Argentina and was training battalions of Hitler-clones in preparation for a world conquest. Another dark and terrifying story said he was the Hollywood executive responsible for *"Independence Day."*

Huck never heard from Hunsey again after the boy drove out of Humboldt County in what was left of the Bourcartemobile. Over the years Huck had occasionally visited Hunsey's father, Chick Bourcarte, the old man who fed the chimpanzees at the Centerton Zoo. Huck would stop by at the zoo to chew the fat with old Chick and the two of them would sit in the aviary and break the rules by feeding the birds. Old Chick looked amazingly like his main charge, a Chimpanzee named Will (who, at 62, was almost as ancient as the man). It seemed appro-

The Marriage Proposal

priate, since Chick had always spent a lot more time with the ape than he ever had with his wife or son. The wife (now deceased) had eventually divorced him and married a sales rep from Cleveland. The son, Hunsey, had eventually taken to spending more time in jail than at home.

As they tossed pieces of Twinkies™ and Ho-Hos™ to the ground for the diet-challenged birds, Huck would ask Chick for any new addresses or telephone numbers that might help him to reach Hunsey. Sometimes Chick had a little new information, sometimes he didn't, but either way Huck had never been able to contact Hunsey again. Currently, in the corner of his refrigerator chalkboard, he had seven different addresses for the lousy Judas.

Still, he decided to try inviting Hunsey to the bachelor party. If it didn't work, well, Bubba's bachelor party committee was out a few invitations and some stamps. If it did, Huck would be able to show Hunsey the letter he'd received from Miss Felecia Vandermark. Two could play at that game.

So a few hours later Huck dropped the bachelor party invitations into the postal box at the main post office, including seven that were addressed to Hunsey Bourcarte's last seven known addresses.

Huck had only one other item to take care of before he started tackling the rest of his bachelor party planning duties. He had to buy a wedding gift. He wouldn't have remembered it on his own, but he'd overheard Little Larry talking about it. It wasn't a big deal or anything, but if he didn't do it right away he was going to forget it again. Luckily he had an ally in the battle to find a gift; The miracle of the wedding gift registry.

Registries were a godsend as far as Huck was concerned. Without them a person had to actually think about what to purchase, and thinking had never been Huck's strong suit. With a registry all a body had to do was go into the store, pick something off the list that nobody else had bought the happy couple yet, and then put down the first layaway payment. Registries also shifted the blame for selection of the gift to the recipient (i.e., the bride) and saved the gift-giver from embarrassment later on when the bride traditionally objected to a Beer-Of-The-Month-Club subscription as inappropriate.

Roberts' was one of Huck's favorite and least-favorite stores to browse. On the one hand, the store smelled great. The scent of herbs, cinnamon, and spices from the potpourri baskets next to the bread machines mingled with the scent of the gourmet coffee beans in the bins behind the espresso makers so beautifully that Huck sometimes walked the isles just to sniff the air. On the other hand, the place was terrifying. Towering displays of delicate crystal teetered just inches from collections of imported porcelain figurines. Dangling metal windchimes swung perilously close to cabinets filled with fine china. Huck had never understood the term "bull in a china

The Marriage Proposal

shop" until the first time he'd wandered into Roberts'. Just to be on the safe side he'd taken to just coming in the front door, standing on the store's welcome mat sniffing the air, and then leaving before he could get into any trouble.

So on this particular day Huck made a beeline from the front door to the wedding registry counter and got Pat, a really nice lady who worked the counter, to check off a gravy boat from the list. She wrote up a layaway tag (he'd be able to pick it up no later than a week after the wedding), he dug a crumpled ten out of his pocket, got a receipt, and then plotted a course straight for the door with his hands in his pockets.

That was when he heard the conversation.

In the next aisle over Faith Heisler and Alverna Kettle were talking. Huck stopped suddenly in front of the crystal garden gnomes when he heard the words "...Bubba..." and "...mercy and sakes alive..." He ducked down a bit and stroked a gnome, pretending to be shopping. It was a natural response, considering his years of neighborhood watch training and his natural predisposition to eavesdrop.

"I tell you, I have seen that Cheryl Wingate before, and she wasn't always Cheryl Wingate," Faith was saying. Faith, who worked at the District Attorney's office, knew just about everything about everybody in Humboldt County, and what she didn't know Alverna Kettle, the town's manager of gossip and malicious hearsay, certainly did.

"Well, you know she just came back from Los Angeles," Alverna replied, suggesting with her tone that there was absolutely no hell worse to have just returned from. "I hear she was trying to get work there as a *model,*" she added, suggesting that this attempt to deal with the devil said all that needed to be said about the woman.

"No, no, I mean when she used to live here before," Faith argued. "I processed some paperwork with her picture, but the name was different. I think she was much slimmer then."

"Poor dear tips the scales now," Alverna sighed. "That's those models. They all have eating disorders."

"Cherry Rodriguez!" Faith suddenly exclaimed. "That was it! Leona Rodriguez' maiden name was Wingate. She's just gone back to using her mother's maiden name! And right she should after that monster Len Rodriguez left the family high and dry. She's Cherry Rodriguez!"

The blood drained from Huck's face and the world went cold.

VIII
Tales Of Humboldt Babylon
In which the Hollywood tabloids are bested by Humboldt County

While Huck Puhzz, our general main character and usual starting point, is busy sticking his head and arm into the main post office's postal box - committing a federal offense while trying to retrieve his brother Bubba's bachelor party invitations - let me tell you a story.

Back in the old days, before Huck had gotten his job pulling chain at the mill but after he'd dropped out of high school and restored McKinleyville's honor by dropping Centerton's statue of the dead President into Old Man Frerichs' outhouse, he spent most of his days eating Jolly Rancher candies and smoking cigarettes down by the waterfront with his best friend, Hunsey Bourcarte. The two boys were practically inseparable. Every time a sheriff's deputy stopped one of them on suspicion of knocking over mailboxes with a baseball bat from the Bourcartemobile's passenger window on a Friday night he stopped the other, who was sitting behind the driver's wheel. Whenever one was caught hauling a dumpster to the roof of 2nd & K Liquors, well, the other could always be located at the far end of the rope. If one was seen in the trees across from the girls' dormitory at the college the other one was certainly hiding in the bushes. No two delinquents have ever been so firmly attached at the hip.

But one night Hunsey decided to discard all of that, leave his old life and move on to a new one. No one knew what catalyst drove him to abandon everything he knew. However, most people were fairly sure it was Cherry Rodriguez.

Cheryl Rodriguez was a debutante that summer, with a big society coming-out party at the Centerton Oddfellows' Hall (which her very busy father actually attended) and her picture in the newspaper (which her very busy father even clipped out). All those extra pounds Cheryl had carried through grammar school were now gone thanks to participating in her mother's latest diet-of-the-month fad (the cabbage soup plan). She'd recently graduated from the Little Miss Professional Finishing School (which she attended after her classes at St. Bonafice High School and before the tutor arrived to help her with her homework.)

Harvard, Yale, and several other notable colleges were vying for her attention. She'd asked her father Len, the very busy attorney, which school he would recommend. He didn't seem to have a preference. Catherine Wingate-Rodriguez, Cheryl's mother and a loan specialist at Mad River Bank & Trust, wrote to her old college counselor to find out which school was currently in fashion. Cheryl asked her father what sort of work or study he would recommend for her to do over the summer in order to prepare for her senior year, but he very busily told

The Marriage Proposal

her that she should do whatever she wanted. Her mother went to the library and researched what careers were currently most promising for upwardly-mobile women.

What I mean to tell you, I guess, is that everything seemed to be going just peachy at the Rodriguez household until Cheryl's father ran off with the lady who fixed the copiers at his law office.

Her mother did not handle the abandonment well. She took to shaking and calling everyone "Larry," then quit her job and checked herself into a very nice recovery center called Peaceful Glen (yes, they'll help people recover from anything as long as your health plan covers it.)

Cheryl fared even worse, though. The second night after her father flew to South America she got out of bed just after midnight, yanked on a pair of jeans and a t-shirt, and ran crying into the night. She continued running until she wound up in the middle of US 52 and then she started walking straight down the yellow line in the dark. When two bright headlights rose like the sun over the hill and almost blinded her she just kept walking. It was only luck that when Hunsey Bourcarte slammed on the brakes he stopped two feet shy of her kneecaps.

"What the hell, girl, are you trying to get yourself killed?" he'd asked her.

"Maybe," she'd answered. Hunsey thought about it and decided that "maybe" wasn't too unreasonable an answer, so instead he invited Cheryl to ride along with him. For her part, Cheryl was out of breath from running and figured that getting a free ride wouldn't hurt. For his part, Hunsey figured she was pretty good looking and so far tonight had been a bust. So she'd jumped into the Bourcartemobile and he peeled out and raced down US 52 toward town.

"So why 'maybe?'" he asked her.

"Why not?" she responded. "My parents don't care whether I'm alive or dead anyway."

"Who cares what they think? You care whether you're alive or dead, don't you? I mean, you can't really change that you were born. You can't change that someday you're gonna die. But you can sure as hell enjoy what comes in between," Hunsey said.

Cheryl didn't respond at first, and then she whispered, "How?"

"What?"

"How can you enjoy being alive when no one else cares?"

"You *make* them care."

A grin that would have frozen better men's hearts spread across Hunsey's face. Very few of the people in Humboldt County enjoyed life quite the same way Hunsey Bourcarte did. The few who did spent most of their time in Sheriff Wadd's jail cells. Even his best friend, Huck, usually asked to be dropped off at home when he saw that expression on Hunsey's face.

The Marriage Proposal

"I'll show you how, babe," he said. "Good God, I don't know your name. What's your name?"

"Cheryl. Cheryl Rodriguez."

"Hmmm," Hunsey thought for a moment. "Not nearly good enough. I'm going to call you Cherry."

The tale of the night that followed has been recounted many times in conversation, in newspaper stories, and in high school poetry classes throughout Humboldt County.

Hunsey started things rolling by getting his Dad's chainsaw and cutting down two telephone poles located just east of the electric company's switching station. When the poles went down so did the electricity, and McKinleyville - and most of Centerton - were plunged into darkness. Between the power outage and the overcast-moon-and-star-free sky, Hunsey figured the rest of the night would go much easier.

After that they drove up to Kneeland Mountain and herded two of Jim Richardson's cows into the pickup bed of the Bourcartemobile. Once back in town they released the poor animals smack dab in the middle of the Centerton town square. The cows milled about in the dark intersection and were spared being turned into steak by late-night motorists only through several strokes of good fortune. Hunsey strapped a note on the west side lamppost with duct tape. He smiled as he showed it to Cherry. It read;

"You live like cattle, you can deal with cattle. Sincerely, Hunsey Bourcarte and Cherry Rodriguez."

Moving uptown, Hunsey liberated a hose from the volunteer fire department and they ran it from a nearby fire hydrant to the outside air circulation intake on the roof of Haley's Department Store (the management there had refused to hire Hunsey twice.) He and Cherry stood at the front windows and waited just long enough to see water begin to rain down onto the sales floor from the vents in the ceiling before they drove off north through town.

"Well, I'm certainly enjoying life," he told Cherry.

Next they stopped at the BIG MALL 6 movie theatre. Hunsey took the ladder he kept clamped on the side of the Bourcartemobile up to the marquee and began to rearrange the letters that spelled out the movie titles. He tried "FART ZONE" and "FOR ALL IZ A SHIT LIFE," but neither slogan satisfied him. The available letters limited their choices somewhat and the two delinquents studied them carefully. Then Cherry spoke up.

"Life is a horizontal fall," she said.

Hunsey laughed and spelled it out. "That's good. Did you think of that?"

"No. Jean Cocteau."

"Jacques Cousteau?" he called out to Cherry from the top of the ladder. She started to speak and then stopped. "The old fish guy?"

"Never mind," she said.

The Marriage Proposal

"Enjoying life yet?" he asked.

Around three-fifty they finished gathering up about twenty newspaper-vending machines that contained the *Cross-County Weekly*, a tabloid which consisted primarily of thirty-six pages of classified ads. Growing up, Hunsey had hated the little piles of the free paper that always built up, unsolicited, on the front porch and lawn. More than once he'd had to pull soggy pieces of newsprint out of the mower blades after running over one of the damned things. So tonight he and Cherry dumped the towering pile of vending machines on the front lawn of the adzine's publisher. "See how he likes it when people dump unwanted garbage on his lawn," Hunsey said.

Their exploits took them near Hunsey's house, so he stopped by his garage for some paint. One by one the two of them climbed onto the dozen or so billboards which lined the highway between McKinleyville and Centerton and painted their own messages across them. They started with Cherry's "Life is a horizontal fall," which then inspired Hunsey's "Life is what happens to you while you're busy making other plans." ("John Lennon said that," Hunsey pointed out. "He was a much better singer than Jacques Cousteau. But not as good a SCUBA diver.") Half-way through Hunsey remembered another brilliant aphorism and added "Tomorrow is the first day of the rest of your life." Beneath the slogans on each and every billboard they signed their work, writing in big dripping red letters "courtesy of Hunsey Bourcarte and Cherry Rodriguez." The last two signs were especially hard to read because it had started to rain.

By the time they snuck out of the rain and into KHUM, the all-night oldies/talk/news/jazz/folk/alternative rock/interesting-stories-told-by-Cliff station, their fame had already begun to spread. The station was still on the air thanks to a generator, and Hunsey and Cherry creeped into the lobby around five o'clock in the a.m. The morning drive people, who'd just arrived for the day, were still taking doses of coffee in the break room, so the only person actually working was Marty the graveyard guy. In fact, Marty was just finishing the local news.

"So, power should be restored by nine or ten, folks," he reported. "The vandals responsible for the outage, who've brazenly left messages confessing to their criminal acts, are still at large and a manhunt has begun for them."

"See? Suddenly they all care," Hunsey said to Cherry. "We're still at large right here," he added much louder as they entered the booth. Some DJs might have been alarmed by an 'at-large' criminal mastermind breaking into the air booth, but Marty had gone to school with Hunsey and wasn't scared in the least.

"Ladies and gentlemen... and Sheriff Wadd... we've just been joined in the KHUM studio by the culprits in last night's rampage of destruction, confessed lawbreakers Hunsey Bourcarte and Cherry

The Marriage Proposal

Rodriguez. Hunsey, what's the story?" Marty, somewhat tired after a long shift, handed the microphone to Hunsey and leaned back in his chair to smoke a cigarette.

"I don't know really, Marty. I guess I'm just here to say 'Life is what happens to you while you're busy making other plans.' And... what was the other one, Cherry?"

"'Life is a horizontal fall,'" she answered.

"Right. 'Life is a horizontal fall,'" Hunsey said. "Those are our messages."

"They aren't very original," Marty pointed out.

"No," Hunsey admitted.

"Do you have anything to add, Miss Rodriguez?" Marty asked Cherry. She paused, thinking. People very rarely asked her for her opinion on anything. But here she was on live radio, dozens of early-risers waiting to hear what she had to say.

"Mom, I'm not going to college to study how to be a snob," she started slowly, leaning into the mike. Then her voice rose. "You and Dad don't care about me, so I don't care what you think either."

"Obviously a very complex sentiment," Marty said. "Hunsey, aren't you concerned that the sheriff will be here any minute and that you'll be arrested for what you've done?"

"No," Hunsey said calmly, standing. "I put potatoes in all the deputies' tailpipes." And he asked Cherry, "Enjoying life yet?"

"Yup," she smiled. They left the booth.

But they weren't quite finished yet. Hunsey still had one more thing to do before he discarded his old life. He had a friend to say goodbye to. As they went out, Cliff-in-the-morning came into the booth from the opposite end cradling four cups of steaming coffee.

"Who was that?" he asked.

The sun was starting to rise as Hunsey and Cherry finished their hike up Cobb Mountain, but it was hard to tell considering the dark rumbling stormclouds that covered the sky. They stopped just beneath the electric company's reflector dish which sat atop the peak. It was upon this very spot that Hunsey and his best friend Huck Puhzz had committed their very first act of social rebellion. Just four years earlier the two comrades-in-disaster had climbed this peak and painted over the reflector to honor their final days in High School. Granted, it had been an imperfect job (they got caught because Hunsey had left a few tools on the scene, all of which were clearly labeled 'Bourcarte'). But it had been a special moment in Hunsey's life, up here on the mountain with his amigo, working closely together toward a common goal like brothers are supposed to do. Smiling at the memory, Hunsey dropped the huge, ancient CB radio and car battery he'd lugged all the way to the top.

"Why, again, are we here and why did you

The Marriage Proposal

bring that?" Cherry asked.

"After what we did last night I'm going to have to leave town... and I've got one last loose end to tie up," Hunsey said.

"You're leaving town? Can I come?"

"Natch," Hunsey smiled, and he powered up the CB radio. Holding the outsized microphone to his lips he called out, "Breaker breaker! Beep to Huckleberry! Beep to Huckleberry!"

And then lightning struck them both.

Really. That's what happened. What can I tell you? Fate is sometimes cruel.

Hunsey Bourcarte never finished his CB call to his old friend and Huck never knew his buddy had even tried. The paramedics took Hunsey and Cherry to the emergency room where both remained unconscious for several days. The town's power system was restored, Haley's Department Store was mopped up, the cows were hauled to Kneeland, and the billboards were repainted. Cherry's mother called the doctors from her retreat at Peaceful Glen and told them to call her if her daughter ever woke up. Sheriff Dennis Wadd became embroiled in an election controversy and, despite the severity of their crimes, the district attorney set aside the charges against Hunsey and Cherry. After all, he couldn't very well prosecute the two pitiful vegetables who now lay in the Humboldt County Community

Hospital.

Pretty sad end, huh? Well, don't get your panties in a bunch, because there's one last bit.

Two and a half weeks later Doctor Putney stopped in to check on his patients and found their beds empty. Twenty-six hours after that, newly-elected Sheriff Freedom Kearney discovered that the Bourcartemobile was missing from the impound yard. A brief note had been left in its place: "Life is an experiment without results. We're off to try something new. Love and kisses, Hunsey Bourcarte and Cherry Rodriguez."

What can I tell you? Fate sometimes has a fine sense of irony.

IX
The Bachelor Party
In which many erroneous assumptions are made

The bachelor party being thrown for Bubba Fitzgerald Puhzz was pretty successful at first. It isn't hard to throw a good bachelor party, after all. Only three things are required; guys, entertainment (girls), and alcohol. This party definitely had all three. The attendees showed up at the Elks' Hall around nine and started drinking, and the strippers waited in back for a signal from Larry that the guests

The Marriage Proposal

were ready for the show to begin.

Out in the main hall Big Kenny was seated next to Bubba, slapping him on the back and keeping him well-watered. Guys who barely knew Bubba but who'd come for the showgirls and beer were congratulating him and telling ribald jokes. There was a boom box hanging from the center light fixture that was pounding out AC/DC so loud that a 747 could have snuck through the hall at full throttle and no one would have heard.

Huck sat alone in the corner. Oh, he was still happy about his long-distance love-letter love affair, but that was in a shoe box at home and Bubba's big deal was right here, live, with about forty friends and acquaintances and enough cheap booze to keep a battleship group afloat for a week. Besides, he hadn't gotten a second letter yet from Ms. Felecia Vandermark, and he was beginning to think that the Best Supporting Actress Nominee of 1986 had already forgotten about him. He was trying to feel good about all of this for his brother's sake, but he found that it wasn't easy to set aside his natural sibling rivalry considering the circumstances.

"Guess Hunsey didn't get none of them cards?" Hampton said, coming over to break Huck's solitude out of pity.

"Nope," Huck said. Huck hadn't expected the turncoat to show up even if he did.

"Probably for the best, considering," Hampton pointed out and then, noticing his glass was dry, he headed back to the bar. Word had spread throughout town, thanks to Alverna Kettle - the gossipmonger of McKinleyville - that Bubba's bride-to-be, Cheryl Wingate, was no less than the infamous Cherry Rodriguez, the nefarious moll of that criminal mastermind, Huck's former best pal, Hunsey. Cheryl modestly claimed her ways were mended and Bubba had accepted that, but the town was less forgiving.

Sammy and Little Larry were sitting a few feet away from Huck, trying to see how many empty beer bottles they could fit on a single table. Of course, they had to make them empty by drinking the beer first.

"All this sudden getting married stuff," Little Larry said, just after slamming a cold one, "I don't buy it. You don't just marry whoever comes along. You won't find me settling that way. For me it's going to have to be absolute true love."

Sammy shook his head. "That's what you always believe at your age, boy. No such thing as true love. Only truly love."

"What?" Little Larry came back.

"You'll never find true love, only truly love. True love is a myth... what you'll actually do is marry some girl you sorta like and then, at some point after you've been together about ten or twenty years, you learn to truly love her."

"That's depressing," Little Larry said.

"Yup," Sammy admitted.

The Marriage Proposal

Joe Bosanfari stood over at the drinks table pouring something amber-colored into the fruit punch. He might have saved his whiskey if he'd known the punch was already two-thirds alcohol. But Joe had been the official class "punch spiker" throughout High School and it was tough breaking those old habits. Not far away, Chet Fisher handed out lollipops shaped like women's breasts and other unmentionables, which he considered a bachelor party staple.

The music was suddenly shut off and then the floor was brought to order by Cranly Davin. Cranly was a professional local celebrity. He was especially good at unrehearsed and spontaneous nonsense, talking at length about how wonderful it was to "be" someplace or how nice the weather was today. Every time there was a parade you could find Cranly on the judges' stand, microphone in hand, identifying the various floats for the crowds and dazzling the public with his in-jokes about the community leaders who went by slowly in ribbon-festooned convertibles. Every time there was a telethon for Jerry's Kids or the Cancer Society he would be there hosting on the TV screen, introducing in his lounge-singer cadences the High School rock band acts and the aging torch singers who had gotten most of their experience at the Karoke bar. Many people thought that Cranly went on and on just because he liked the sound of his own words, but others suspected he was attracted by the influence his notoriety gave him. At big McKinleyville Rotary functions you could find him telling all the best jokes and schmoozing with Mayor Victoria Fletcher and the Sanders brothers at the power table. He had achieved a fairly high-profile position, by association and by grandstanding, in the Humboldt community. But, to tell the truth, no one was quite sure what it was that Cranly Davin did for a living.

"A toast! A toast to the groom!" Cranly called out, and then surprised Huck by turning toward him and saying, "How about you make it, Huck?"

There was a moment of almost-silence (amazing, considering how much liquor had already been imbibed.) Huck really wasn't in the mood to salute his brother. He looked up from his drink.

"A toast? I didn't prepare a toast," he said.

"Be extemporaneous," Cranly advised. Huck didn't know what 'extemporaneous' meant, but he could see that he was still expected to make the toast.

"All right, for God's sake." He stood, wobbling a bit. "I don't know," he mumbled, "I guess... good luck, happy life, have lots of kids and all that crap." Then he knocked back his drink in a single gulp. The room paused. The posse looked toward Bubba for instruction.

"HA!" Cranly suddenly exploded. "'All that crap!'" he guffawed, "You're such a card, Huck!" and then he raised his glass and drank. The room broke into a moment of laughter (which quickly subsided to make room for alcohol intake) and then the noise

The Marriage Proposal

resumed. You see, there was a reason Cranly Davin got all those master-of-ceremonies gigs. He could handle a crowd like butter.

Bubba remained in particularly good spirits. Cheryl's assurances that she'd left her life as Cherry Rodriguez back in L.A. along with her modeling career had satisfied him. After all, if she was still a law-breaking tramp she certainly wouldn't have agreed to marry a fine upstanding citizen like him. Big Kenny, who was by now very drunk, was draped over Bubba's left shoulder crooning loudly, "I love you, man! You're the absolute best, man!"

Fritz Gibson came up to Bubba and told him, "My boy, not only are you now in retail management, but you're going to be a married man too! You've become a responsible member of the community! I suppose it's time you joined the Rotary... can you come to our meeting next Wednesday?"

Damn, Huck really hated this party.

It was only going to get worse. In just a few minutes would come the strippers, and everyone would stick twenty dollar bills in their skivvies and tell them to go sit on Bubba's lap (but no one, of course, would send one over to sit in poor Huck's lap.) The only way Huck was going to get out of this evening without shooting himself (figuratively speaking, of course - do not try this at home) was if a miracle occurred.

I bet you see it coming, don't you?

Yup, a miracle occured. Alverna Kettle

showed up at the door.

"Stripper do her thing yet?" the nosy woman asked, peeking in and sniffing at the air.

"Get out of here, Alverna, this is for men only," Larry said, barring the door. Alverna smiled wickedly.

"That's what they said over at the bridal shower, down at the Chinese Baptist Church. 'Women only,' they said. But wouldn't you know it, there's a man there anyway." She smiled again and started to turn away, but she'd got a line out in front of Larry and he took the bait.

"Who?" he demanded.

"That fella that Cheryl used to consort with. Hunsey. Hunsey Bourcarte."

Larry told Bubba a few seconds later. Huck didn't find out until Alverna Kettle, who had snuck in after the initial shock of the announcement cleared the front door, made her way over to him and gave him the news herself.

"That Hunsey Bourcarte is at the bridal shower tryin' to steal away your brother's fiancée. I don't suppose he bothered to tell you he was coming? You, his old best friend?"

That Alverna, she always did love to see a good set-to.

The story spread around the room quickly, whispered from one partygoer to the next and growing with each telling. "Cheryl's old boyfriend,

The Marriage Proposal

Hunsey Bourcarte, is at the Bridal Shower," said the first guy to the second, who passed on, "Hunsey Bourcarte is with Cheryl at the Bridal Shower" to the third, who said "Hunsey and Cherry are dancing together at the Bridal Shower" to the fourth, who told a small group next to him "Hunsey is having sex with Cherry on the dance floor at the Bridal Shower."

The normally laid-back Bubba didn't react at first. His face warmed a bit, his jaw set a fraction. Then he stood, his arms trembling slightly at his sides. Then his breath came out in a slow hiss.

"Boys, go home and get your guns. I'm gonna kill 'im!"

"What about the strippers?" Joe Bosanfari asked as the last man vanished out the door.

"The Church's windows were all open to allow the evening breeze to circulate the air inside, so the twenty-three women attending the celebration heard the roar of the engines as thirty-seven drunken men carrying shotguns, rifles, and six-shooters drove at excessive speeds toward them with nothing but murder in their minds."
      page 209

X
Dear John
In which secrets are revealed and new possibilities arise

It was a warm summer night in June in the rural town of McKinleyville. A group of middle-aged women who served as the permanent rotating High School Reunion committee and also organized bake sales for the local library had arranged a bridal shower for hometown girl Cheryl Wingate (who had recently returned from Los Angeles) at the Chinese Baptist Church. The Church's windows were all open to allow the evening breeze to circulate the air inside, so the twenty-three women attending the celebration heard the roar of the engines as thirty-seven drunken men carrying shotguns, rifles, and six-shooters drove at excessive speeds toward them with nothing but murder in their minds. This horde consisted of former revelers at Bubba Puhzz's bachelor party, where the rumor had started that the bride-to-be's ex-boyfriend was chatting her up down at the shower. Grooms-to-be are notoriously jealous.

The parade of vehicles screeched into the Church parking lot and stopped willy-nilly in-between the other cars, blocking them in. Reverend Kim, who had heard the cars and trucks from his house behind the church, ran into the lot and tried to keep the "fire lanes" clear, but he was uniformly ignored by the drunken throng (much as he was by his congregation on Sundays.) Huck parked his truck out on the highway and dodged his way between the late arrivals on foot.

Bubba and Big Kenny were the first of the mob to enter the Church. The women, who had been seated opening presents, had all stood to look out the window (except six-foot-four-tall Horsefeathers Snoqualmie, who could see out of them from her seat.) Now they all turned to stare at red-faced Bubba. Their eyebrows rose, as if to ask, "Yes?"

"Hey, darlin', what are you doing here?" Cheryl asked.

"I'm looking for that no-good Hunsey Bourcarte, that's what," Bubba spat. He shook his rifle in the air and Reverend Kim ducked behind the buffet table.

"Why?" Cheryl asked, genuinely confused.

"That's cute! He's jealous!" Betty Jean Essex said, and the women all laughed. Well, they laughed until Bubba took a shot into the ceiling. The sharp crack of his rifle echoed in the room for a few moments and quite a few faces went pale.

Reverend Kim crawled out the door on all fours.

"Where is he?" Bubba demanded.

By now the rest of the men had gathered next to him, forming a line that paralleled the women on the other side of the room. Sorta like High Noon or the O.K. Corral, but the women weren't armed.

The Marriage Proposal

Huck pushed his way between Hampton and Larry to stand at the front next to Bubba.

"C'mon, Bubba, this just isn't gonna work," he started to warn his brother. "You're just gonna get thrown in jail..."

It was at this precise moment, in-between the word "jail" and the next word, which Huck intended but never uttered, that a cry went up from amongst the women.

"Huck!"

An incredibly gorgeous woman, tall and slender with long flowing blond hair, moved gracefully from the center of the group. Even Bubba temporarily forgot his mission and lowered his rifle as this beautiful creature stepped forward. She wore a tight minidress that emphasized her ample breasts (with generous cleavage visible) and exposed her long, shapely legs. The men all took in a short breath as she walked over to Huck, high heels clicking on the hardwood floors. Huck's gaze was swallowed by her dark raven eyes, then shaken loose as she batted her long lashes. She stopped directly in front of Huck and reached up and took his collar.

"Hello, Huck," she said. And then she kissed him passionately on the lips.

When they parted, Huck stood there for a moment in a daze. He used his sleeve to wipe the lipstick from his mouth. Staring at the dazzling woman in confusion, he tried to figure out how he'd gotten so lucky. Then, suddenly, everything fell into place. His eyes grew large and he turned and ran from the Church, doubling over with one hand across his stomach as if he was going to be sick.

Cheryl walked over to the line of men, putting her arm around Bubba, and called after him.

"Hey, Huck, aren't you going to say hello to Hunsey?"

Once he stopped wretching in Reverend Kim's tulip beds, Huck made his way back into the Church. The men had set aside their weapons and were now dancing with the women. It seemed, at least as far as Bubba and the posse were concerned, that there were only women at the bridal shower after all. Joe Bosanfari brought the strippers over from the Elks' Hall and, dressed in nothing but their G-strings, they enjoyed the food and company. He'd also brought the boom box, and they'd cleared away an area by the emergency exit so that they could dance to the music. Bubba and Cheryl were sitting together on the couch making smoochie faces at one another. Apparently she had found Bubba's jealousy flattering.

It took a while before Huck was willing to sit down on the couch (on opposite ends with plenty of buffer zone in-between) to talk with his old friend Hunsey. It turned out Hunsey hadn't gotten any of the invitations Huck had mailed. Instead he had received an invitation to the bridal shower from Cheryl, who still exchanged Christmas cards with him.

The Marriage Proposal

Hunsey now went by the name Georgia Shetley and lived in San Francisco. He/she broke down and cried when he/she recounted his/her adventures after dropping Cherry off at the bus station in Oakland on the same night they escaped from the hospital.

"So," Huck finally gathered the courage to ask, "what's with the dress and stuff?"

"All those things Cherry and I wrote all over town, they were all just nonsense," Hunsey said sadly. "I was just angry, mad at the world because I didn't know what my life was all about. Then that beautiful bolt of lightning struck me and all that nonsense got scrambled into the truth."

"What's the truth?" Huck asked, doubting it was anything as simple as 'dresses are more comfortable on a hot day.'

"What I wrote on that last note. Life in an experiment, but there are no results. You never get it perfect. You just experiment and keep trying to make things better until you're dead. I mean, even the oldest person on Earth hasn't gotten it perfect yet. Realizing this liberated me."

"You became a liberal?" Huck asked.

"No, you goof," Hunsey scolded. "I stopped letting other people tell me who I was supposed to be, and started experimenting more."

"You got it perfect yet?" Huck asked, rather earnestly.

"No. But I've gotten it much better." Hunsey laughed and tugged at his long blond hair. "I'm so sorry things turned out the way they did, Huck. I always wanted to say goodbye to you, and then later I thought about calling you. But I'd been changed so much by that night..." Tears began to form again in Hunsey's eyes. "I'm so glad we have this chance to make things right. Let's never lose touch again." He leaned over and his hand came to rest on Huck's knee.

Being a natural-born homophobe, Huck began to panic.

He was saved by the last person he expected. Suddenly a great shadow passed over him (and over Hunsey as well.) In silhouette Huck could see long flowing tresses of jet black hair cascading out of a giantess' furry black cossack's hat. Her long, lacey black chenille dress fell almost to the top of her rugged black combat boots. In-between the dress and the boots an inch or so of black fishnet stockings could be seen. The only light in the ebony of her form radiated from her ivory skin and her pale blue eyes.

"Horsefeathers?" Huck said.

"Huckleberry Samuel Puhzz, would you like to dance?" she asked.

Between the horror of Hunsey's hand on his knee and the terror of being embarrassed on the dance floor with Horsefeathers (who was, at least, an actual woman), Huck decided on the dancing. Of course, he'd always sort of been sweet on Horsefeathers anyway. Ever since High School his

The Marriage Proposal

still-teenaged libido had been mightily aroused by Horsefeathers. They'd had "The Lunch" which had led to "The Kiss." But gentlemen don't kiss and tell, especially when the kissee is a Snoqualmie, so it had all ended right there.

"Sure, thanks," Huck said, but to keep from sounding too eager he added, "I guess."

Hunsey tugged on Horsefeathers' dress before they could leave for the dance floor.

"Horsefeathers..." he said, batting his eyelashes and then tugging at his own dress, "remember when I called you an 'ostrich-lovin' zombie girl'?"

"Yeah," Horsefeathers said. Huck remembered too.

"I'm sorry," Hunsey apologized. "Really, I was just jealous of your fishnet stockings."

"Well, that's okay," Horsefeathers smiled. "It wasn't an altogether untrue statement, although the ostriches in question were emus."

As Huck and Horsefeathers started walking away Hunsey called after Huck.

"Hey, Beep!" The voice sounded so much like the old Hunsey that when Huck turned back he almost expected to see a lanky teenager clad in denim overalls instead of a drop-dead blonde in a bright red minidress.

"Yeah, Hunsey?"

"Experiment, Beep," Hunsey smiled. "Don't forget to experiment."

As Huck's luck would have it, just as they arrived on the dance floor the DJ slipped on a slow one and Horsefeathers pulled him in close. Neither one of them was brave enough to lead, so they just sort of swayed in a circle. The top of Huck's head was about even with Horsefeathers' chin, which offered him a view he didn't altogether mind.

"So, has that actress written you back yet?" Horsefeathers asked as they danced.

"Nope. But she will, you bet on it," Huck replied.

"Is she eloquent?" Horsefeathers inquired.

"What?"

"Did she write well?"

"Oh, she used a lot of hundred dollar words, if that's what you mean. You'd expect that, though. She's refined."

"Ah," Horsefeathers agreed as Huck stepped heavily on her foot. "That makes all the difference then." She turned her head and rested it on the top of his. He could smell the dusty-sweet scent of the emus in her hair. "You want to get lunch together tomorrow?" she asked.

"Nah, I gotta stay home and watch my mailbox," he said, moving back and forth with her to the rhythm of the music.

"Oh," she sighed.

An hour or so later Horsefeathers went home to feed the emus, so Huck helped Bubba and Cheryl

The Marriage Proposal

haul all of the gifts and leftover food and booze from both parties across the highway and up to Bubba's cabin. It turned out that Hunsey had wandered off earlier, arm-in-arm with a friend of Bubba's from the bowling league who may have come in late and missed some crucial information about his companion.

After things had pretty much died down and most of the people had gone home, Sheriff Kearney - who had responded to Reverend Kim's frantic phone call and then stayed to dance and drink - helped run off the posse and the other drunks who were asleep or passed out on the church pews. After that he took the strippers home in his cruiser (whether it was to their home or his home wasn't made clear.) When the Kims locked up the back door of the church the first rays of the morning sun were already creating a halo over the mountains to the east.

It was better than half past four in the morning when Huck pulled up to his driveway. Out of a habit built up over the last month he automatically checked the mailbox, even though he'd just looked at six the previous evening. To his surprise there was a letter. It had no return address on it (in fact, there weren't even any stamps) but the handwriting was unmistakable. Huck's mind had been so preoccupied by the events at the Chinese Baptist Church he had almost forgotten the Best Supporting Actress Nominee of 1986. But here was the response he'd been waiting for.

After driving the truck into his yard and parking in front of the trailer he ripped open the envelope and started to read.

> Dear Mister Huckleberry Samuel Puhzz,
> Your letter has touched me in more ways than you know. I was also fascinated by your account of the life of Augustus Caesar. However, it has become clear that you are far too good for the likes of me. Years of living in this city of sin have taken their toll. No one succeeds here without giving in to the depraved movie star lifestyle of sex and drugs that the tabloids so accurately chronicle. I am nothing more than a Hollywood harlot, and I beg you to turn your attentions to a nice, wholesome local girl, and give up any fascination with me. I pray for your salvation, although my own soul is surely lost.
> Yours sincerely,
> Felecia Vandermark

Huck sat in the car for a while, staring at the side of his almost-a-mobile-home and trying to form thoughts. Finally, he clambered out of the truck and climbed the steps to the front door and let Whizzer in. It was so late the hound dog didn't even offer his customary whine.

Once inside Huck sat down at the kitchen

The Marriage Proposal

counter (brushing away the empty tins to make room - Merry Cunningham's neighborly offerings had switched from preserves to pies.) He read through the letter from the Best Supporting Actress Nominee of 1986 one more time. In the back of his mind (which was pretty near the front) he could hear Andy Peterson's near-to-last words; "I figure I gotta meet somebody soon. Hell, I'm forty-two."

Don't want to die single.

"Well, Hunsey, I guess I'll just have to experiment," Huck said to himself quietly.

He pulled out an expensive fountain pen and a piece of the new scented stationery he'd bought at Pacific Paper Company & Office Supply and started to compose a letter.

Dear Ms. Vandermark,
　You aren't no harlot,

And in his very best cursive penmanship he added;

and I don't think you're depraved neither... I think you are one of the most considerate people I ever have met. Plus you kiss great, and I've always really loved that little peek of fishnet stocking between your dress and your boots.

　Yours Sincerely,
　Huck Puhzz

"After driving the truck into his yard and parking in front of the trailer he ripped open the envelope and started to read."
   page 218

Epilogue

Well, for the moment that's all I can relate to you concerning that particular subject. Or, at least, that's all that Huck and Bubba have actually told me thus far.

You see, for me all this started when I was tooling down Highway 52 a few months back on my way to the Redwood Coast Jazz Festival. It was late and I was tired, so I stopped off in Centerton for a drink at this place called Khartoum. Khartoum is a bar, but not your average we-don't-want-to-go-home-so-we're-sitting-here-like-zombies-smoking-and-drinking bar. It's sort of like Disneyland. The owners have fixed up the inside of the place to make it look like a marketplace in ancient Egypt (or, at least, a Disneyland-type interpretation of a marketplace in ancient Egypt.) The walls are covered in stucco and there are mummies' coffins and strange hieroglyphs carved in the beams. The windows are all stained glass with brightly colored pictures of camel trains, pyramids and the sphinx, and a huge faux thatched roof extends from above the bar. In the midst of all this sits the clientele, most of whom don't want to go home and are sitting there like zombies smoking and drinking.

There weren't any free tables the night I walked in (this being a Friday), so I asked two gentlemen near the front window if I could sit at their table in the extra chair. They politely grunted in assent and one of them pushed the chair out with his foot. I introduced myself and they said they were brothers by the names of Huck and Bubba Puhzz. Huck seemed somewhat agitated.

They looked as if they were between thirty-six and forty-one years of age - the both of them - of medium height with brown hair and bluish eyes. They weren't thin, but then they weren't too heavy either. Both wore blue jeans and green denim shirts, with big ol' Timberlands on their feet. I ordered what they were currently drinking - a dark beer called Downtown Brown, but from the collection of empty glasses - of many different sizes and shapes - I guessed they liked variety.

"Interesting town," I told them, mostly just to break the uncomfortable silence while I waited for the barmaid (a guy named Dave) to return. At least they had their beers to suck on.

"This town is absolutely crazy," Huck contradicted with passion. Something was definitely sticking in his craw this evening. "I mean, they... well, they... well, damned if I'm not the only sane person in it." He turned to his brother, red-faced. "Except you, Bubba. My apologies."

He turned back toward me and poked the air with his finger. "I swear, you don't know *half* the tales I could tell," Huck said.

At first I considered moving to another table, but then my Wiser Voice spoke up and pointed out my habit of squandering opportunities. Instead, I

Epilogue

smiled at Huck and took a sip from the delicious beer the barmaid dropped in front of me on the table. "No, but I'd sure like to hear you tell them. I really enjoy stories. I'm a writer, so I sort of collect them. Want to tell me a few?"

"You're a writer? You mean like Bob Thalia?"

"Yeah, I guess."

"It'd take a while," Huck said, eyeing the empty glasses and then conspicuously checking his equally empty wallet. I pulled out mine and tossed three twenty-dollar bills onto the table (the old-style ones, not those new ones that look like Monopoly money.) Their eyes bugged out, I swear. I think Bubba's eyes popped even more than Huck's.

"I'm buying," I said with a smile. I love storytelling. I love hearing stories and reading stories almost as much as I love telling stories and writing stories. An evening's entertainment was worth a sawbuck or six.

"You gonna tell other people these stories? You know, write 'em down and stuff?" Huck asked, suspicious.

"Maybe. Depends. Of course, if you don't want to share them with me, I understand completely," I said, and I reached out and started to scoop up my money. Bubba gave Huck a look that would have melted the Wicked Witch and saved the water.

"No, no," Huck said, tapping the back of my hand and pushing it away from the bills on the table. "Just curious, that's all. I don't mind telling."

So as the barmaid returned for round after round, bringing beers, Irish coffees, and something called Lynchburg Lemonades (Bubba's favorite), Huck told me a variety of tales, some of which I have passed on to you in the preceding pages with very little embroidery. At appropriate moments Bubba threw in a comment, more often a single word like "Yup." Only at last call, perhaps six hours later, did we finally part, and I drove my Bronco out into the rain.

Pretty wild stories, I thought to myself as I chewed gum to the cadence of the windshield wipers. Whup-whup-whup. Pretty odd town. Pretty crazy county.

Of course, Huck probably made the whole thing up.

The End

Huck Puhzz will return.

About The Author

Perry Bradford-Wilson lives in Humboldt County, California, and swears that every word of these stories is fiction... sort of. He is the co-publisher of a monthly humor magazine titled *Comic Relief* (12-issue subscriptions are available for $35 from Comic Relief, P.O.Box 6606, Eureka, CA 95502 - hey, you have to get these plugs in where you can!), and he owns J.J.Perry's Books & Video, a not-quite-for-profit bookstore in Eureka. He likes to read, go to the movies, SCUBA dive, waste hours by the dozen on the internet, and write really silly stories. Perry is also, regretfully, still single and looking for his own personal Horsefeathers.

Perry is diligently waiting for his next two much-more-serious novels, *Storyteller* and *Memory*, to finally finish writing themselves. He has also started letting the next "Tales Of McKinleyville" story, titled *The Little Bears Go To Vienna* (or something like that) ooze forth from his subconscious.

About The Photographer

Brandi Easter is a professional photographer in Humboldt County and owns Brandi Easter Photography, P.O. Box 962, Arcata, CA 95518. Perry talked her into doing this, so don't blame her.

> This book is a work of fiction. Although the names of some actual counties, cities, and locations are used, they are always used fictitiously. All other names, characters, places, and incidents are products of the author's imagination. Any resemblance to actual events or persons, living or dead, is entirely coincidental.

Acknowledgements

About three years ago I wrote a very moving dedication intended for my first novel. I'm saving it for a serious I'm-shootin'-for-a-Pulitzer type book. Here I'd like to thank the usual suspects;

A Special Thanks to

Bradford P. Wilson (the best Pa on the planet), Joy Lynn Wilson (author of about seventy-five unpublished manuscripts), Orpha Frerichs, Joanne Hankins, and The Hardy Boys for getting me interested in this writing thing at the right time in life.

Also, many thanks:

To Brook Wilson (no, you! no, *you!*), Crystal Breazeale and Bob Breazeale for being there even when they're very far away.

To Michael Norris for the many great unfinished projects, unpublished stories, and unfilmed screenplays we've brainstormed together. I'm sure some idea fallout from those collaborations occurs here. Mike - our partnership means a lot to me! Tell Gina (aka Wendy) her name is here too.

To Roseann Viano for still talking to me after 1986 (and for simultaneously inventing the phrase "Big Doin's At The Chinese Baptist Church" when we observed unusual midweek activity at the Chinese Baptist Church in Campbell, California.) Muotrahk.

To Alan Johnson and Dallas Brunson for bits, pieces & ideas culled from days & nights at the Lost Coast Brewery.

To Cyndi Christopher for insulting me because I am the world's best procrastinator. Well, here it is!

To Michael Kunz and Kevin Fox for putting up with my absentmindedness and keeping the businesses running.

To Mike Cunningham for making me think people might actually laugh at this stuff.

To David Baker for being such an absolutely great Dave.

And, of course, to Keela, my ghostly muse from midnight until three a.m. every night at the Eureka!-I-Found-It Coffee Shop.